BRITISH AIRPORTS

4th EDITION

ALAN J. WRIGHT

LONDON

IAN ALLAN LTD

Contents

First published 1979
Fourth edition 1991

ISBN 0 7110 1971 1

Published by Ian Allan Ltd, Shepperton, Surrey; and printed by Ian Allan Printing Ltd at their works at Coombelands in Runnymede, England

Front cover:
An Iberian A300B4-203 Airbus seen at Bristol (Lulsgate) in December 1984.
Aviation Picture Library

Back cover:
A Shorts 360 of Loganair.

Acknowledgements

Grateful thanks are extended to BAA PLC, the Directors and staffs of the many independent airports, the Civil Aviation Authority and the patient and helpful bus enquiry office staff around the country. Of the many individuals who have helped in some way, special thanks must go to George Pennick, Allan S. Wright and Colin Wright.

Introduction

In these modern times air travel has become an essential part of everyday life. Businesses often depend upon the swift movement of personnel for transactions to succeed, while millions take holidays which would be impossible without this mode of transport. Nevertheless it is the availability of airports which makes it all a practical proposition. Few people actually acknowledge the important part played by these complexes and certainly pay scant attention to the multitude of facilities provided to ease the fear, irritation or boredom. Undoubtedly some terminal buildings are more pleasant places than others, but generally most offer a considerable amount of interest and entertainment if only to observe the arrivals and departures. Students of human behaviour can find it absorbing to watch the antics of passengers in charge of baggage trollies that resist all forms of control.

Non-travelling visitors are catered for with varying degrees of understanding. In some cases arrangements are extremely good, but unfortunately the trend is moving away from such accommodation, leaving few official vantage points from which the tearful can wave and the curious can watch. No one expects or needs an elaborate seated area with high-class catering provided, but a simple enclosure situated in a reasonable spot helps to keep spectators away from the already congested terminals. With space at a premium and the need to contain costs, the authorities do not have an easy task to meet the requirements, but it is not impossible.

Sadly, security has become an essential feature at all airports, resulting in the appearance of substantial chain-link fences. While this necessary obstruction does not affect viewing to any great extent, photographs usually become more difficult to obtain. Since the orders to erect this entry deterrent were issued by a government department, it is unlikely that the civil servants responsible considered any cheaper but effective alternatives.

In addition to the lofty barriers, there has been a significant increase in the number of security officials on patrol. Most of these carry out their duties in a sensible and understanding manner, but there are others who are completely inflexible and obsessed with the new-found power provided by their uniform. Usually, the method adopted for wearing the peaked cap gives a good indication of the likely attitude, with those resembling an SS officer the most intolerant. Nonetheless all are employed for a good reason and it has to be accepted. Interestingly, the authorities at military bases are now far more amenable and often provide special areas for viewing and photography.

It is hoped that this book will be of use when planning a trip to UK airports. The main section includes those handling scheduled services with the exception of some of the islands off the British coast. Due note should be taken that the inclusion of a particular operator against an airport does not guarantee the appearance of its aircraft. Carriers have a habit of changing routes from time to time and it is not unknown for them to disappear completely with little warning. A typical example of such an occurrence is the failure of Air Europe in March 1991. Even ground transportation has become affected by similar practices, causing well known and long established bus companies to acquire new names, liveries, route numbers and in many cases the adoption of minibuses instead of the lumbering double-deckers used hitherto. For this reason no attempt has been made to mention costs because these can also change regularly usually to become more expensive. When contemplating travelling any distance it is always advisable to check that the spectator facilities are open. Only too often some international squabble such as the Gulf crisis or a sensitive airline can result in closed doors with little or no advance warning. Ironically these precautions have not prevented acts of terrorism, none of which have been perpetrated from the confines of a viewing gallery or enclosure. Security checks as performed at some major European airports such as Zürich and Frankfurt would seem a positive solution, at the same time reducing any perimeter fence congestion by parked cars. It must of course be emphasised that entry into unauthorised areas of any airport or airfield is forbidden. Prior permission should always be sought in writing before visiting individual airlines or companies.

Key for Map

1	Wick	25	Ipswich
2	Inverness	26	Stansted
3	Aberdeen	27	Luton
4	Dundee	28	Gloucester/Cheltenham
5	Glasgow	29	Heathrow
6	Edinburgh	30	London City
7	Prestwick	31	Southend
8	Carlisle	32	Kent International (Manston)
9	Newcastle	33	Bristol
10	Teesside	34	Cardiff
11	Belfast (Aldergrove)	35	Gatwick
12	Belfast (City)	36	Lydd
13	Isle of Man	37	Shoreham
14	Sheffield	38	Southampton
15	Leeds/Bradford	39	Bournemouth
16	Blackpool	40	Exeter
17	Liverpool	41	Plymouth
18	Manchester	42	Newquay
19	Humberside	43	Penzance
20	East Midlands	44	Land's End
21	Norwich	45	Isles of Scilly
22	Birmingham	46	Guernsey
23	Coventry	47	Jersey
24	Cambridge	48	Bembridge (Isle of Wight)

Abbreviations

A/G	Air-ground communication station
AAC	Army Air Corps
ABC	Air Bridge Carriers
AEF	Air Experience Flight
APP	Approach
ARRS	Airborne Rescue and Recovery Squadron
ATI	Aero Trasporti Italiani
A&AEE	Aircraft and Armament Experimental Establishment
BA	British Airways
BAF	British Air Ferries
BEA	British European Airways & Birmingham European
BIA	British Independent Airways
BOAC	British Overseas Airways Corporation
BR	British Rail
CAA	Civil Aviation Authority
CAF	Canadian Armed Forces
CFS	Central Flying School
CTA	Compagnie de Transport Aérien
DAT	Delta Air Transport
EFTS	Elementary Flying Training School
E&RFTS	Elementary and Reserve Flying Training School
FAA	Fleet Air Arm
FIDO	Fog Intensive Dispersal of (also known as Fog Investigation & Dispersal Operation)
Flt	Flight
FSS	Flying Selection School
FTS	Flying Training School
IT	Inclusive Tour
IWM	Imperial War Museum
JAT	Jugoslovenski Aerotransport
KIA	Kent International Airport
KLM	Royal Dutch Airlines
LOT	Polskie Linie Lotnicze
MCA	Ministry of Civil Aviation
MHz	Megahertz
MOD	Ministry of Defence
MU	Maintenance Unit
NLM	Nederlandse Luchtvaart Maatschappij
OCU	Operational Conversion Unit
OTU	Operational Training Unit
PR	Photo Reconnaissance (Unit)
RAE	Royal Aircraft Establishment
RCAF	Royal Canadian Air Force
Reg	Region
RFG	Regionalflug
RFS	Reserve Flying School
RLG	Relief Landing Ground
SAR	Search and Rescue
SAS	Scandinavian Airlines System

STOL	Short take-off and landing	TWR	Tower
TAP	Transportes Aereos	TWU	Tactical Weapons Unit
	Portugueses Air Portugal	TWCU	Tactical Weapons Conversion
TAT	Transport Aérien Transrégional		Unit
TEA	Trans European Airways	UAS	University Air Squadron

Aberdeen (Dyce)

Passenger services were started at Dyce in 1934 when Aberdeen Airways opened a route to Glasgow using a Short Scion and de Havilland Dragon. The following year a service to Edinburgh provided the oppor- tunity to connect with the London flights of North Eastern Airways. The airline later became known as Allied Airways, by which time extensions to the route network took in the northern islands in addition to Wick and Inverness.

The RAF was in evidence at Dyce by

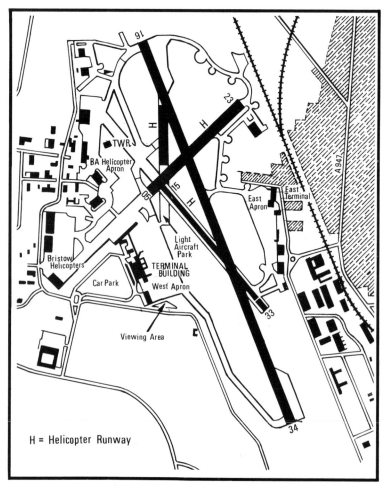

1937 when No 612 Squadron was formed. Initially it was equipped with Hawker Hinds but it was not long before Avro Ansons were on strength. The airfield was requisitioned in 1939, whereupon hard runways were laid for the use of Coastal Command squadrons. Dyce also saw a little civil flying during the war when it was used as the UK terminal for some of the transport services to Sweden.

After the war civil flying was resumed alongside that of the military, scheduled services being undertaken once again by Allied Airways until in 1947 the operations came under the control of BEA.

Expansion was slow with services few until the North Sea oil activity began to have effect. It soon became the fastest growing UK airport, passing to British Airports Authority control on 1 January 1975. Plans were rapidly put into effect to greatly enlarge the facilities, which resulted in a new terminal building, taxiways and apron areas being constructed for a 1977 opening.

Aberdeen also became one of the world's most active bases for helicopters engaged in oil support work. Charter operators were also kept busy, the carriers changing as the contracts came up for review. British Airways uses a mixture of Boeing 737s and Airbus A320s on the lucrative Heathrow route, while Dan-Air provides services to Gatwick with One-Elevens and BAe 146s. The number of destinations available for travellers has steadily increased, several routes being flown by foreign operators. However, in the mid-1980s a decline in the off-shore gas and oil industry became apparent, which in turn began a reduction in the number of charter operators active at Aberdeen. Nevertheless the airport still handles a considerable number of movements.

Location and access: Situated 7 miles northwest of Aberdeen on the A96 from which it is signposted. Charges graduated at both the main and heliport car parks. A Grampian Transport bus runs between the airport terminal and Aberdeen bus/rail station at half-hourly intervals in peak periods and every 40min at other times. These also call at the heliports every day except Sunday. Journey time is 30min. It is necessary to produce the exact fare on boarding. The east terminal reached via the A947 is used by some helicopter operators

Terminal: Main building is a modern structure containing Aerogrill, bar, buffet, shop and waiting area

Spectator facilities: None are provided in the terminal. There is a viewing area situated to the south of the building from where it is somewhat poorly signposted. It is necessary to walk along the front of the complex past the cargo sheds until a set of concrete steps are found. Once at the top a path is followed to the spectators' area. Admission is free. The spot is an excellent vantage point for viewing activity on the apron and runway. Photography is possible through the substantial 10ft fence; a notice proclaims the authority's regret at having been forced to instal this standard obstruction.

Operators: Scheduled services by Aberdeen Airways (BAe 748, Gulfstream 1). Air France (Boeing 737), Air UK (Friendship, BAe 146, Short SD3-60), British Airways (Boeing 737, Airbus A320, BAe 748/ATP), Business Air (Bandeirante, Short SD3-60, Saab SF340), Business Flight (Metro), Dan-Air (One-Eleven, BAe 146), Gill Air (Short SD3-30), Muk Air (Bandeirante), SAS (DC-9)

Charter and IT operators: Aberdeen Airways (BAe 748, Gulfstream 1), Air Malta (Boeing 737), Aviogenex (Boeing 737), Britannia (Boeing 737), British Air Ferries (Viscount), Brymon Airways (Dash Seven), Dan-Air (BAe 748), Spanair (DC-9), British International Helicopters, Bond Helicopters, Bristow Helicopters

Movements (1989): Total 104,410 (air transport 75,656/club 10,213/test & training 11,860/empty positioning 4,479). Total passengers 1,758,334

Runway: 16/34 (6,000ft/1,829m). Used only by helicopters 01, 05/23 and 15/33

Belfast International (Aldergrove)

The airfield was first used in 1918 although it was not developed until the outbreak of World War 2. During this time it had become the home of No 502 (Ulster) Squadron, which operated initially as a night bomber unit, converting after 10 years to a day bombing role before, in 1938, it took on reconnaissance duties with Coastal Command. Throughout the war various squadrons spent time at Aldergrove either to engage in patrols over the Atlantic or anti-submarine duties. These operational units were joined by No 23 Maintenance Unit late in 1939, which thereafter handled such types as the Wellington, Hampden and Blenheim. The airfield was also chosen to receive the first deliveries of the American-built Hudson, the pioneering seven flying across from Newfoundland. After the war regular Met flights were flown by No 202 Squadron equipped initially with Halifaxes, this type being replaced with the more modern Hastings in 1950. It was an essential duty which was to last until mid-1964. During this period the Ulster auxiliary squadron was in residence equipped with the Mosquito, Spitfire and lastly the Vampire, before the unit was forced to disband in 1957.

Until 1963 the airlines had used Nutts Corner for their Belfast operations, but space on the site was so limited that expansion was not practical. On 26 September all services were moved to Aldergrove which had been rebuilt as Northern Ireland's gateway. When it opened the airport possessed a brand new modern terminal complex incorporating the now familiar pier loading system. It has since been developed to enable it to handle transatlantic movements, although for many years this traffic tended to use Prestwick, passengers being ferried across the water by connecting feeder flights. This practice has now ceased with North American ITs originating at Alder-

grove although the airport still has no schedules on this route.

Like the two Scottish cities, Belfast has a shuttle service to London flown by British Airways. With the retirement of the Trident in December 1985, the trunk route was taken over by Boeing 757s, but with some timings in the hands of the smaller 737. Competition on this route is supplied by British Midland's DC-9s and 737s, while until 1991 Dan-Air offered an alternative London terminal by using Gatwick for its One-Elevens and 146s. On the debit side, Aldergrove lost some of its commuter traffic to Belfast Harbour from February 1983, the latter being situated much nearer to the city centre.

Any deficiencies in total traffic are expected to be restored by the increased amount of freight handled by the airport. At the beginning of 1991 a new £7 million cargo complex with its own dedicated terminal and associated offices was due to open. An apron extension was included in the development to accommodate the latest Boeing 747-400 freighters which will be a common sight in the future. During 1989 the throughput of freight totalled 35,000 tonnes which was carried by an average of 35 flights per day and 17 at night. As the number of European and long-haul destinations increase, so Belfast International will be firmly established as a main gateway.

Location and access: Situated 13 miles northwest of Belfast on A26, 4 miles south of Antrim. Car park charges graduated. Buses run half-hourly from Great Victoria Street bus station to the airport with a journey time of 40min
Terminal: Contains bar, restaurant, self-service buffet, shops and lounge area
Spectator facilities: No specific viewing area provided. Movements can be seen from the first floor departures level which overlooks the apron
Operators: Scheduled services by Air France/TAT (Fellowship), Air UK (Friendship), British Airways (Boeing 757, One-Eleven, BAe 748/ATP), British Midland (DC-9, Boeing 737, BAe ATP), KLM CityHopper (Fellowship), Britannia Airways (Boeing 737), Birmingham European (One-Eleven)
Charters and IT operators: Adria Airways (DC-9), Air Atlantis (Boeing 737), Air Europa (Boeing 737), Air Transat (TriStar), Aviogenex (Boeing 737), Balkan (Tu-154), British Airways (Boeing 757), British Air Ferries (Viscount), British Midland (DC-9, Boeing 737), Dan-Air (One-Eleven), Inter European (Boeing 737), Lineas Aéreas Canarias (MD-83), Spanair (MD-83), Viva Air (Boeing 737), Worldways (TriStar, DC-8).
Numerous freight flights are operated by a variety of carriers including Air Bridge (Merchantman), Loganair (Short SD3-60), Woodgate Air Services (Navajo), Gill Air (Short SD3-30), British Air Ferries (Viscount)
Movements (1989): Total 95,670 (air transport 35,860/club 16,187/military 32,657/positioning 5,395). Total passengers 2,164,564
Runways: 07/25 (9,111ft/2,777m), 17/35 (6,400ft/1,951m)
Radio frequencies: 118.3MHz (Tower)/ 120.0MHz (Approach)/ 120.9MHz (Radar)
Telephone: Belfast (08494) 22888
Operated by: Northern Ireland Airports Ltd

Belfast City (Harbour/Sydenham)

When some reclaimed land in Belfast harbour became available, the opportunity was taken by Harland & Wolff to construct a new yard for its shipbuilding activities. Later an aerodrome was built alongside the premises and the company moved into the aircraft business in association with the Rochester-based Short Bros. Although ideally situated, the somewhat soggy nature of the surface was not suitable for commercial operations when it was completed in 1933, but following the erection of a large factory by the owners, new drainage schemes rectified the problem. Officially opened on 16 March 1938 by the Prime Minister's wife, the new site soon attracted airlines away from the other Belfast airport at Newtownards.

Aircraft production started in 1936, with the newly created Short & Harland given the task of building Bristol Bombays, Blenheim sections and the in-line engine version of the Hampden known as the Handley-Page Hereford. Shorts had secured the contract to supply the RAF's first four-engined bomber which was to become known as the Stirling. Production of the new type at Rochester was painfully slow, so to speed matters a new line was installed at Sydenham, with work on the first batch starting in June 1940. It continued until eventually more than half of the 2,381 machines produced had been built at the Northern Ireland site.

By this time the airfield was under the control of the RAF and was used by squadrons employed in the city's defence. From November 1941 the airfield took the name of RAF Belfast, but with an increasing presence by naval squadrons it was inevitable that in June 1943 another change found it with the identity of HMS Gadwall. Ideal facilities existed for ease of loading carriers since the airfield was alongside the docks. For this reason the base was also the arrival point of vast numbers of American-built warplanes that were shipped across the Atlantic. Unloaded from the decks of the cargo vessels, the machines were quickly test flown before delivery to the maintenance units on the mainland.

After the war Shorts converted Sunderlands and Seafords into civil transports, while in the 1950s the company became involved in building some of the Britannias for Bristol after the Sydenham runway had been extended to 6,000ft in 1952. Original Short Bros designs were built and flown, the most impressive being the giant Belfast freighter which sadly attracted no orders other than 10 for the RAF. In the 1960s the company's efforts were directed into the Skyvan, later developed into the 30-seat SD3-30 and the larger SD3-60 commuter airliners, both proving very popular with the smaller airlines, particularly in America.

Commercial operations were carried out at Nutts Corner after the war, but, while suitable for the airliners of the day, the larger types coming into service in the late 1950s needed more space, something that the air-

port could not offer. Accordingly Aldergrove became Belfast's airport in September 1963, providing all the modern facilities demanded by the new equipment and travelling public. However, in 1983 Short Bros was persuaded to reopen its airfield at Belfast/Harbour (as Sydenham was now known) to commercial traffic. Blackpool-based Spacegrand became the first airline to move to its Irish terminal, quickly followed by others such as Loganair.

Growth was rapid as travellers came to realise the advantages of its position close to the city centre. At first almost all services used either the SD3-30 or 3-60, although on occasions the Viscount appeared at peak times. Thereafter the number of routes available gradually grew until by 1990 they equalled those offered by Aldergrove. Several, such as Manchester and Leeds, were in competition, the passengers' choice usually depending on whether onward flights were involved. Until mid-June that year, five operators (Manx, Loganair, Jersey European, Gill Air and Capital) shared the traffic using Friendships, SD3-30/3-60s and BAe 748/ATP/146s. The total number of carriers was then reduced by one following Capital's difficulties towards the end of the month.

Needless to say the loss of business was not popular with the Aldergrove authorities who usually object to any new proposal for services from its near neighbour.

Location and access: Situated directly beside a main dual carriageway 2 miles from the city centre on east side of Belfast docks. Journey time by road is 5min. Alternatively there is a rail station 100yd from the terminal which is reached by using the footbridge provided. NI Railways operates frequent services to Belfast Central taking only 5min to complete the journey. A Citybus service leaves the station forecourt every 30min on weekdays (40min at weekends) on a circular route which takes in East Belfast and the city centre.
Terminal: Contains buffet and bar
Spectator facilities: None provided. Vantage points can be found on the perimeter
Operators: Scheduled services by Jersey European (Friendship), Loganair (Short SD3-60, BAe ATP/146, Jetstream), Gill Air (Short SD3-30), Manx Airlines (Short SD3-60, BAe 146, Jetstream)
Movements (1989): Total 28,872 (air

transport 19,187/test and training 2,468/military 5,832). Total passengers 506,993
Runway: 04/22 (6,000ft/1,829m)
Radio frequencies: 130.75MHz (Tower)/ 130.85MHz (Approach)/ 122.45MHz (Radar)
Telephone: Belfast (0232) 457762
Operated by: Belfast Harbour Airport Services Ltd

Bembridge (Isle of Wight)

In the early 1920s a landing ground was created on ground belonging to a local farm. For many years it was used by private aircraft visiting the Isle of Wight, but in the mid-1930s Spartan Air Lines operated scheduled services into the airfield although its merger with United in 1935 brought an end to the venture. At this time there were more popular airfields at Sandown, Ryde and Cowes, each of these being included in various route networks before the war and even into the 1950s.

Nowadays Bembridge is far better known as the home of Pilatus Britten-Norman and the Islander family, but in the 1980s there were several attempts made by carriers to restart regular flights to the island. While these efforts to introduce schedules so far have been unsuccessful, a local tour operator, Bath Travel, operated its first charter flight to Jersey in September 1985 using an Islander for the return trip. The programme was expanded in the two years that followed when the increased number of flights were maintained by a 14-seat Trislander operated by Aurigny Air Services. Due to popular demand, even more capacity was necessary in 1988 and 1989 which was achieved by employing an 18-seat Brymon Twin Otter for the sorties. Finally Bath Travel arranged to charter a Dash Seven from London City for its short season in September 1990, the 44-seat type being the largest commercial airliner capable of using Bembridge. Special Customs services have to be provided since none are normally available at the airfield. Two series of flights were planned for 1991 (spring and autumn) once again using the Dash Seven, but this time in British Midland's livery.

Location and access: Situated alongside the B3395 Brading-Bembridge road, 1 mile southwest of the latter
Terminal: Refreshments can be obtained at the Propeller Inn
Spectator facilities: None provided. Views of all activities are possible from the perimeter
Operators: Charter services by British Midland (Dash Seven)
Movements (1989): 9,044 (air transport 76/test and training 1,797/club 6,440). Total passengers 662

Runway: 12/30 (2,746ft/837m)
Radio frequency: 123.25MHz (Tower)

Telephone: (0983) 872511
Operated by: Pilatus Britten-Norman Ltd

Birmingham (Elmdon)

Plans to establish a municipal airport were initiated by the City Council as early as February 1928, but another eight years passed before construction began. The distinction for becoming the first aircraft to land on the newly-laid grass went to Western Airways' DH90 Dragonfly registered G-AEDH, but it was on 1 May that the airport opened for business. This time it was the Swallow G-ACXE which was the first arrival, having transported the Lord Mayor from nearby Castle Bromwich for the occasion. Later that day the inaugural scheduled service was handled when a Rapide of Great Western and Southern Airlines touched down after its trip from Liverpool and Manchester. Following the customary addresses by the civic authorities, the machine was allowed to resume its journey south to its next stop at Bristol en route to Southampton and Ryde. As it left, the assembled guests were given a second chance to indulge in some harmless pomp when the four-engined DH86 G-AEFH arrived. Operated by Railway Air Services, it was on its regular journey to Liverpool and Glasgow. Nevertheless some work was still outstanding on the terminal building, while levelling of the 800-acre site continued. Another two months of intensive work completed the initial phase of the undertaking and on 2 July the first foreign commercial movement was recorded when a KLM DC-2 arrived from Schiphol. There were three grass landing strips available, each 3,000ft in length, with a fourth earmarked for use in conditions of bad visibility since it was 900ft longer. Six days later Elmdon was formally opened by the Duchess of Kent and operations began in earnest.

At the beginning of the war No 14 Elementary Flying Training School (EFTS) was established, Tiger Moths thereafter becoming the resident landmarks for over six years as control of the airfield had been assumed by the Air Ministry on 16 September 1939. Not only was Elmdon suitable for flying training, but it also became the flight test centre for Stirlings and Lancasters built by Austin Longbridge. Assembled at the Marston Green shadow factory, they were then towed for their aerial baptism from the short-lived airport. Demob came on 19 June 1946, but instead of reverting to Birmingham Council it became the responsibility of the Ministry of Civil Aviation. For some time flying was restricted to club or charter movements, but after representations to the authorities, BEA eventually launched a scheduled service to Paris in partnership with Air France on 8 April 1949. At last the Midlands had a regular link with the Continent and it was joined shortly after by both Swissair and Aer Lingus operations.

It was not a time of rapid growth for the aviation industry, so notable events were scarce during the airport's early postwar years. However, there was one highlight on 22 December 1954 when a Sabena DC-4 landed after a transatlantic flight, the first such movement for Birmingham. While its arrival did not create any major difficulties, it did serve to illustrate the future trend.

Impatient to regain its long-lost possession, the Council submitted a request to the Ministry once more, but as on previous occasions a firm rejection was received. Undeterred, the city's authorities persevered until finally on 1 April 1960 the battle was won: Birmingham had its airport again after nearly 21 years. As some form of compensation an improvement grant was awarded to provide a much-needed extension to the terminal, which was duly opened by the Duchess of Kent on 28 April 1961.

During its requisitioned time the site had benefited by the provision of two hard runways, one of which had been extended to 5,000ft (1,562m) prior to the handover in 1960. Further lengthening in 1967 took the main strip to 7,400ft (2,255.5m) making it possible for the economic operation of the modern types then entering service. This brought the need for more terminal expansion, new Customs hall and more space for the bar and buffet. Despite all the work it was not long before there were signs that congestion was returning as the number of passengers passing through steadily increased.

There was no scope for extending the existing terminal yet again, so plans were made to build a brand new complex elsewhere on the site. After prolonged discussions and enquiries the scheme was authorised allowing work to commence in April 1981. Designed to cater for three million passengers and 33,000 movements annually by 1990, the new terminal was positioned on the northeast side of the main runway. Ideally it should have been incorporated with Birmingham International railway station, thereby providing a single integrated unit, but the extensive earthworks and other restrictions ruled the idea out on cost grounds. As a result a 600m transit system was installed to link the two buildings. It was 4 April 1984 when the long-awaited day arrived and the new facility was ready for business.

First scheduled flight away was the Birmingham Executive Airways Jetstream G-OBEA which left for Zürich followed by G-AVGP, a One-Eleven of British Airways bound for Aberdeen. In accordance with tradition there was an official ceremony at a later date, this time undertaken by HM the Queen and Prince Philip on 30 May. A plaque recording the event was unveiled in the entrance, the Maglev transit system later receiving the Royal seal of approval when the couple took a ride to the National Exhibition Centre. Meanwhile, the airport's traffic figures began to reflect the vast improvements as the airlines introduced new services in response to the demand.

Both 1987 and 1988 returned a passenger growth rate of 25% so an £11 million project to provide more accommodation in the terminal was begun. After the opening of the new buildings in 1984, the disused passenger building site had been adopted for freight handling. In view of the steady increase in this business, plans were also made to provide additional facilities starting in 1989.

During the same year, work began in conjunction with British Airways on a £50 million development to provide a specially-designed hub terminal. Located on the extended apron to the east of the domestic pier, the latter was due to be demolished as the new building progressed. When operational there will be 10 airbridge-equipped stands available for the exclusive use of BA and Birmingham European.

Since its relaunch at the beginning of 1989, BEA has become a major force at the airport. It has steadily increased the scope of its European network while at the same time introducing jets on the routes previously flown by Jetstreams and Gulfstreams. The carrier intends to further develop its Birmingham hub with schedules timed to connect with feeder services. The airline's Belfast and Newcastle links already offer such opportunities, while it is expected that other carriers will retime their flights where practicable. At last there is a realisation that a convenient alternative to Heathrow or Gatwick is available, a fact confirmed by the impressive passenger figures achieved.

While most of BEA's activities are geared to the business community, the company does operate charters with its One-Elevens.

However, Birmingham acquired its own IT carrier in 1989 when TEA UK was launched with three Boeing 737s leased from its Belgian parent company. Although the travel trade generally was in a decline, the newcomer managed to survive its first season.

Location and access: Situated 6 miles east-southeast of Birmingham on north side of A45. M6 Junction 4 and M42 Junction 6 provide easy access. West Midland bus route 900 connects the airport with the city centre and Coventry, while route 966 serves the needs of those wishing to travel to Walsall and Wolverhampton. There are also other local services available. National Express provides a number of routes to various destinations in East Anglia, the southwest and the northeast. Service 825 calls at the airport on its regular visits to similar locations at Manchester, Luton, Heathrow and Gatwick. There are frequent trains on both local and Inter-City services taking 10min from Birmingham (New Street) and 80min from London (Euston). It takes only 90sec to travel by the Maglev transporter from station to terminal. Rail enquiries (021) 643 2711. Multi-storey car parks for short-term use are situated adjacent to the terminal, while ample open areas are available for longer stays or visitors. Charges vary according to which is used and the duration

Terminal: Contains good refreshment facilities, bar and shops

Spectator facilities: A glass-fronted covered terrace is provided on the upper floor of the terminal overlooking the apron. There is a small charge. Photography is possible with care. A large open grassed area alongside the southern taxiway affords an excellent vantage point for viewing. Due to the need for additional land for the new terminal, some of the space allocated for spectators has been absorbed for the new structure. This in turn necessitated the resiting of the security fence so that it now comprises the normal form of obstruction for photographers. Nevertheless, with care it is still possible to obtain shots through the chain-link barrier. In any case the shadow caused by the wire disappears if using a 200mm lens. There is no charge made for entry. The authorities are to be

congratulated for recognising the need for such a facility and ensuring that it has been retained despite the terminal expansion

Operators: Scheduled services by Air 2000 (Boeing 757), Birmingham European Airways (Gulfstream 1, One-Eleven, Short SD3-60), British Airways (One-Eleven, BAe748/ATP), British Midland (DC-9, BAe ATP), Jersey European (Friendship), Manx Airlines (SD3-60. BAe ATP), Aer Lingus (Boeing 737, Fokker 50), Air France (Boeing 737, ATR-42, Airbus A320), Cyprus Airways (Airbus A310/A320), DLT (Fokker 50), Iberia (DC-9), JAT (Boeing 727), KLM CityHopper (Saab SF340, Fokker 50, Fellowship), Lufthansa (Boeing 737), Sabena/Delta Air Transport (BAe 146, Fellowship), SAS (DC-9), Swissair (MD-80)

Charter and IT operators: Adria Airways (DC-9), Aeroflot (Tu-134), Air Atlantis (Boeing 737), Air Columbus (Boeing 737), Air Europa (Boeing 737/757), Air Malta (Boeing 737), AirTours (MD-83), Air UK Leisure (Boeing 737), American Trans Air (TriStar, Boeing 757), Aviogenex (Boeing 727/737), Balkan (Tu-154), Birmingham European (One-Eleven), Britannia Airways (Boeing 737/757/767), British Air Ferries (Viscount), Caledonian (Boeing 757), Dan-Air (One-Eleven, Boeing 727/737), Inter European (Boeing 737), Monarch Airlines (Boeing 737/757), Nationair (Boeing 757), Oasis (MD-83), TEA UK (Boeing 737), Worldways (DC-8, TriStar)

Freight carriers: Southern Air Transport(DC-8), Air Bridge (Electra, Merchantman), British Air Ferries (Herald, Viscount), Channel Express (Herald, Electra), United Parcels (BAe 146).

There are also a considerable number of private, club and executive movements especially in connection with events at the National Exhibition Centre. Birmingham is used as an alternative by many airlines when weather conditions or disruptive industrial action elsewhere force diversions

Movements (1989): Total 91,763 (air transport 60,782/club 11,028/private 11,329). Total passengers 3,431,445

Runways: 15/33 (7,398ft/2,255m) 06/24 (4,314ft/1,315m)

Radio frequencies: 118.3MHz (Tower)/ 131.325MHz (Approach)

Telephone: Birmingham (021) 767 5511 (switchboard)/(021) 767 7145 (information)

Operated by: Birmingham International Airport PLC

Blackpool (Squires Gate)

The site of the present airport was the scene, in October 1909, of the first flying display to be held in Britain. Scheduled passenger services were started by Blackpool and West Coast Air Service in 1933 when a couple of routes were opened to Liverpool and the Isle of Man using a Fox Moth and a Dragon. These scheduled operations were transferred to nearby Stanley Park in 1937, leaving Squires Gate a quieter place until the outbreak of war.

Due to its position, the airfield was selected by the Air Ministry for development into a standard RAF station with three runways in triangular formation. It was handed over in December 1940 and although various units had lodged at the airfield during the reconstruction period, the first permanent resident was No 3 School of General Reconnaissance equipped with Bothas and later Ansons. The unit was not alone, since various fighter squadrons involved in the defence of the northern cities were also based at Squires Gate from time to time. The occasional visit by a diverted Railway Air Services Rapide also added to the variety.

In addition to its operational and training role, the airfield was also chosen as the site for a large shadow factory for the Ministry of Aircraft Production. Blackpool subsequently played a big part in the production of the many Wellington variants, especially after the bombing of the parent factory at Weybridge.

After the war, training quickly terminated with the station passing to care and maintenance on 10 October 1945. The MCA assumed control in 1946, whereupon charter and air-taxi work was started, particularly by Lancashire Aircraft Corporation. Later this company became one of the airlines permitted to operate scheduled services from Blackpool to such places as Leeds, London, Jersey, Southport and the ever popular Isle of Man. By the mid-1960s international routes had been added, the airlines involved being British United (CI) Airways, Aer Lingus, Autair and Starways. This situation did not last however, with eventually only British Island Airways left to provide scheduled services to Belfast, Dublin, Isle of Man, Jersey and Rotterdam via Manchester. Air UK inherited such a network when the airline assumed responsibility in January 1980, but it was not long before only Jersey and the Isle of Man routes remained active. Some of the licences were taken up in 1981 by a newcomer to the scheduled scene, Spacegrand operating Navajos to Dublin and Belfast. Loganair also introduced a seasonal Belfast sector into its network employing a Short SD3-30 for the purpose. Air UK wound up its Herald maintenance base at Blackpool, transferring the work to Norwich. The facility was taken over by Air Atlantique which for a time based several of its DC-3 fleet at the airport. This type of aircraft was no stranger to Blackpool, since much of the TV series Airline was filmed locally.

Another significant change came in late 1982, when Manx Airlines took over the responsibility for the Isle of Man services. This new company was set up as a joint venture by Air UK and British Midland, each contributing aircraft from their fleets. Further reorganisation found Spacegrand under the same ownership as Jersey European in the mid-1980s. Gradually resources were combined until the former name disappeared, leaving JEA to operate the northern network from Blackpool. The airport has also become the base for helicopters supporting the oil industry in the Irish Sea, resulting in a new terminal being provided exclusively for this traffic.

A considerable number of movements are generated by the local charter and air-taxi companies in addition to the club and private aircraft based at the airport. On occasions commercial diversions are handled, especially when some unexpected strike closes Manchester. At such times it could be said that a larger terminal would be useful.

Location and access: Situated 2.5 miles south of Blackpool off A584 and about 3 miles from the end of the M55 motorway. Daily rate for car parking. A Blackpool Transport service runs frequently to the bus station with a journey time of about 15min. It is also but a short walk from the seafront tram terminus to the airport entrance

Terminal: The small single-storey building contains bar with buffet (drinks machine when closed), shop and lounge area

Spectator facilities: Grass enclosure between the heliport and airline terminals. Through the years it has gradually shrunk in size until in 1990 the fence line prevents clear views of the apron. While it remains a good vantage point for viewing, photography is now more restricted and largely depends on the number and position of light aircraft parked directly in front of the area. Facing south, in the afternoon of bright days the sun can be a problem. This can be overcome by using an alternative spot on the southern perimeter, from where movements on runway10/28 can be photographed using a 200mm lens

Operators: Scheduled services by Jersey European (Friendship), Loganair (Short SD3-60), Manx Airlines (Short SD3-60, BAe ATP), Air Transport Schiphol (Cheyenne) *Charter and IT operators:* Aviogenex (Boeing 737), Janes Aviation (Trislander, Islander, Short SD3-30). Other occasional charters bring 737s and the like to the airport

Movements (1989): Total 86,764 (air transport 9,139/club 56,806/private 12,975/positioning 5,016). Total passengers 133,525

Runways: 10/28 (6,132ft/1,869m), 07/25 (2,854ft/870m), 13/31 (3,524ft/1,074m)

Radio frequencies: 118.4MHz (Tower)/ 135.95MHz (Approach)/ 19.95MHz (Radar)

Telephone: Blackpool (0253) 43061

Owned by: Blackpool Airport Ltd

Bournemouth (Hurn)

The airfield was opened for the RAF on 1 August 1941. Initially the home of the Telecommunications Flying Unit, Hurn was soon brought into use as the UK terminal for long range transport flights by Liberators. In May 1942 the TFU departed, making way for the Whitleys of Nos 296 and 297 Squadrons. The two units were thereafter engaged in intensive paratroop training exercises, later in the year extending their activities to include glider towing.

The USAAF took over in November for the duration of an exercise. As a temporary measure the RAF moved out, No 296 Squadron returning alone just before Christmas 1942. Almost immediately the Whitleys began to be replaced by Albemarles, the

type making its first operational sorties from Hurn. While detached to North Africa, the squadron's place was taken by No 295 Squadron, again in the process of discarding Whitleys in favour of Albemarles. The return of No 296 at the end of 1943 meant that there were three Albemarle units at Hurn since in the meantime No 570 Squadron had been formed.

The airfield was transferred to Fighter Command in March 1944, the troop carriers moving to other bases in readiness for the invasion of Europe. Hurn began a period of intense activity, various fighter squadrons using it for short periods. On 4 August once again the airfield passed to the Americans, this time for the B-26 Marauders of the 397th Bomb Group. It was another short stay, almost marking the end of military occupation of Hurn. The RAF handed the responsibility for the airfield to the Ministry of Civil Aviation on 31 October 1944.

From this date until 1 June 1946, BOAC operated various services from Hurn before transferring its activities to Heathrow and Northolt. The move of the airlines, which included KLM and Sabena, to the new London Airport meant that activity was much reduced. However by the early 1950s Vickers-Armstrongs were installed in factory accommodation to produce such types as the Varsity, Viscount and much later, the One-Eleven.

Scheduled services were reintroduced in the early 1950s with Jersey Airlines becoming the major carrier in those days. Other airlines launched themselves into the business only to fail one by one. Silver City brought its car ferry operation to Hurn, mainly as a result of the unsatisfactory conditions at Southampton. Both Cambrian and BEA were also active at Hurn at this time for similar reasons, but on completion of the improvements at Eastleigh, they resumed their earlier routes.

In 1967 Channel was forced to vacate Portsmouth, turning to Bournemouth as an alternative centre for its Jersey service. This was later inherited by Dan-Air, Hurn also becoming the southern terminal for one of its Link City sectors, although in 1982 this part of the airline's network was transferred to Metropolitan Airways using Twin Otters for the purpose. Sadly the carrier was forced to cease operations in August 1985 by which time Short SD3-30s were replacing the original equipment. Dan-Air continued to provide daily flights to the Channel Islands boosted by extra sorties at weekends, but for the 1987 season the company greatly reduced its operations from Bournemouth, limiting its services to Jersey only on Saturdays and Sundays. This move resulted from the CAA's award of licences to Jersey European which enabled it to start daily flights to the two larger islands early in January. During 1986 Air Camelot provided links with Cherbourg, Bristol and Alderney using Islanders and Trislanders, but these were withdrawn with the demise of the company. Soon afterwards Regency Airways intimated its interest in a similar network, but no services were forthcoming. Early in 1988 newcomer Air Metro announced its plans to fly schedules (subject to CAA approval) on Paris and Amsterdam routes with a target date in June.

This passed without any signs of commercial movements although the company's new Metro was exhibited at the September Farnborough show. It was destined to be the nearest that the aircraft got to potential passengers because its would-be operator was taken over by Ellan-Vannin before any services were offered. The new owner was not convinced by the type's suitability for the sectors envisaged, so it was announced that Jetstreams would be substituted. Start-up was planned for the spring of 1989 with the proposed routes remaining largely unchanged apart from the addition of a link with Manchester. At least Bournemouth gained one new schedule this time because the service was launched when intended using a Navajo for the thrice daily return. Despite all the confident publicity, EVA failed in its bid to introduce European sectors to Amsterdam, Paris and Brussels and after a year even the single domestic service was discontinued. Guernsey-based Air Sarnia bought the airline in the summer of 1990, but within a few weeks this carrier was also forced to cease trading.

All hope was not lost because a new company known as Southern Airways was already actively preparing itself to enter the scheduled scene. The familiar destinations across the Channel were earmarked but the first venture was planned to be a link with Glasgow using a Saab SF340. At least the travellers from the estimated 5.5 million population comprising Bournemouth's catchment area will be able to fly a non-charter service direct to somewhere other than the Channel Islands. Locally-based Channel Express is also familiar with the islands because it flies regular sorties to and from Jersey and Guernsey with freight using both its Herald and Electra fleets. These movements plus the growing number of IT charters available have helped the airport's economy considerably. Fortunately its developing neighbour at Southampton does not want to attract large scale IT traffic so Bournemouth should continue to benefit in this case. Schedules are a different matter because through the years carriers have tended to favour Eastleigh, but all regional airports now have a chance to exploit the growing congestion elsewhere.

Location and access: Situated 4 miles northeast of the Bournemouth/Christchurch/Poole conurbation. The airport is well signposted off the A338 which joins the main A31/M27 some 7 miles inland. Car park charges are graduated and charged on a pay-and-display basis. Buses pass the access road on their way to and from Christchurch but are infrequent

Terminal: The attractive and well appointed building contains a lounge, cafeteria, bar and shop, the latter offering a good selection of aviation books. Work began on the expansion of the arrivals building in 1990

Spectator facilities: Improvements to the terminal has resulted in a pleasant terrace being constructed along the front of the buildings to which entrance is free. This overlooks the apron area providing a good position for viewing and photography, particularly in the morning and early afternoon. It is made possible because of the commendable decision to create a deep grass covered ditch between the public and the restricted area, into which was built the usual high security fence. The result maintains the intended function of the barrier, but allows unobstructed viewing over the top. Full marks for originality. There are also good vantage points along the road bordering the southern perimeter with excellent photographic possibilities, but there is no parking along this section

Operators: Scheduled services by Jersey European (Friendship), Aurigny Air Services (Trislander), Southern Airways (Saab SF340 — planned for 1991). Freight flights by Channel Express (Herald, Electra) *Charter and IT operators:* Air Atlantis (Boeing 737), Aviogenex (Boeing 737), Futura (Boeing 737), Oasis (MD-83). There are numerous movements by school, club, company and privately owned aircraft both UK and foreign registered. Notable amongst these are the Falcons of FR Aviation and the warbird types of Jet Heritage

Movements (1989): Total 105,166 (air transport 7,438/club 63,649/private 17,427/test and training 5,398/military 9,972). Total passengers 131,421

Runways: 08/26 (6,030ft/1,838m), 17/35 (4,483ft/1,476m). There is space within the airport boundary to extend 08/26 a further 1,155ft/350m when required

Radio frequencies: 125.6MHz (Tower)/119.75MHz (Approach)

Telephone: Bournemouth (0202) 579751

Operated by: Bournemouth International Airport PLC

Bristol (Lulsgate)

Broadfield Down was the name allocated to this Air Ministry station, but this was dropped in favour of Lulsgate Bottom. Built in 1939, its planned purpose was to serve as a night fighter base, but in the event it proved unsatisfactory for this role. Instead a Tiger Moth EFTS moved in on completion, remaining until the airfield was temporarily closed to allow the construction of hard runways. Thereafter Oxfords and Masters were employed on training work throughout the war.

For some years after the departure of the RAF, gliders were the sole users of the airfield. However, it was selected to become the new Bristol airport in the fifties, officially being opened on 1 May 1957 after a new terminal block had been provided. The first scheduled service was in fact flown by a Cambrian Heron on 15 April after transferring the operation from Whitchurch.

This airline accounted for most of the scheduled traffic at Lulsgate in the early days, so it followed that when the general slump of 1958 seriously affected Cambrian, the airport was equally involved. Although the carrier began a slow growth the following year, as a precaution the Lulsgate authorities also invited Dan-Air to serve the area. This operator started both domestic and international services from Bristol in 1960, some of the routes flown surviving to the present day. The third airline quickly on the scene was Aer Lingus with a Dublin service, followed in 1962 by a link with the new airport at Cork.

Throughout the 1970s, Cambrian and later its successor, British Airways, served Lulsgate with Viscounts and One-Elevens on a variety of routes including the Channel Islands, Paris and Belfast. However, these were steadily cut back in frequency until in 1980, the carrier terminated its association with the airport. Its departure left all services in the hands of Aer Lingus and Dan-Air, the latter picking up some of the licences recently vacated. One significant change to come later was the successful application by the airline to compete with the Irish carrier on the Dublin run. However, the traffic failed to justify two carriers, in due course leaving Aer Lingus to maintain the route alone once again. In an effort to improve the situation Short SD3-60s replaced the One-Elevens on the services which at the same time were increased in frequency. Dan-Air still flies to the Channel Islands and Belfast, but these are the only two destinations remaining from its once extensive Bristol network. Brymon uses a Twin Otter on its Scilly Isles seasonal service, but the most significant addition to the Bristol schedules was the introduction of links with Paris, Amsterdam and Dusseldorf flown by Air France, NetherLines and DLT respectively during 1986 and 1987.

At the time, however, this type of business only accounted for some 28% of the Bristol traffic, the other 72% coming from the flourishing IT market. All the major tour operators include the airport in their programmes using a mixture of UK and foreign carriers. As the demand increased so there was scope for a new locally-based airline to be formed during 1987. Paramount Airlines subsequently became the first company to use British-registered MD-83s for IT work. To cope with all the extra traffic, a terminal extension phased over six years was begun in the 1980s with the final modernisation work in the public areas completed in 1988.

In the meantime the authorities continued the search for carriers interested in starting new scheduled services at Bristol. An encouraging degree of success was achieved with Jersey European adding Belfast City, Jersey, Guernsey and Manchester routes, while Capital offered Leeds and Glasgow, Aer Lingus extended its Dublin service on to Brussels, at the same time replacing the SD3-60 with Fokker 50s. Sabena also added the Belgian capital to its itinerary at the start of the 1990/91 winter season, in this case contracting the flights to its subsidiary, Delta Air Transport. Bristol had at last acquired a useful batch of destinations with which to attract travellers accustomed to the two-hour trek to Heathrow. There was even more choice available in November 1990 when the airport became the hub for Brymon's new network of routes which included Dublin, Glasgow, Edinburgh and Paris. A further boost was received in March 1991 when Crossair inaugurated a link with Zürich. Fortunately this steady growth compensated for the general decline in IT traffic which began in 1989 with the demise of Paramount.

For many years a point on the Post Office's week-night mail flight network, the airport continues to play host to a Herald of Channel Express during the course of the aircraft's return journey between Bournemouth and Liverpool. Several company-operated machines are based at Bristol which together with those of the local club and private owners, all contribute to the increasing number of movements.

Location and access: Situated 7 miles southwest of Bristol on A38. Car park charges graduated and are payable at a self-service pay station located opposite the terminal. Badgerline bus routes 820 and 821 link Bristol Marlborough Street coach station with the airport, taking 40min for the journey before continuing to Weston-super-Mare. Axevale Coaches' service 490 travels from Temple Meads BR station to Burnham via the airport, while National Express service 731 visits both boarding points in the city before setting off on its 20min trip along the A38.

Terminal: Contains a buffet and bar facilities which now occupy the entire first floor overlooking the apron area

Spectator facilities: Now that the buffet has engulfed the area of roof previously allocated for viewing, a replacement gallery has been provided on the southern end of the building with access via external stairs. While it offers good viewing of all movements, it can become somewhat congested due to the necessity to position the terrace at right angles to the apron. This therefore results in the short side offering the best vantage point, a fact quickly appreciated by the hordes of wavers. The spot also offers good photographic opportunities using a 50mm lens for some of the nearer subjects, or preferably an 80-200mm zoom for those on more distant stands. Mornings and early afternoons best in sunny conditions

Operators: Scheduled services by Aer Lingus (Fokker 50), Brymon Airways (Dash Eight), Air France/TAT (Fellowship, ATR-42), Jersey European (Friendship), KLM CityHopper (Saab SF340, Fokker 50), RFG (ATR-42), Sabena/DAT (Brasilia), Crossair (Saab SF340), Channel Express (Herald — freight)

Charter and IT operators: Air Atlantis (Boeing 737), Air Europa (Boeing 737), Air Malta (Boeing 737), Aviogenex (Boeing 727/737), Britannia (Boeing 737), Cyprus Airways (Airbus A320), Dan-Air (One-Eleven, Boeing 727), Inter European (Boeing 737), JAT (Boeing 727, DC-9), Spanair (MD-83), Worldways (DC-8)

Movements (1989): Total 71,156 (air transport 13,730/club 41,600/private 10,955). Total passengers 869,000

Runways: 09/27 (6,598ft/2,011m) 15/33 (1,627ft/496m)

Radio frequencies: 120.55MHz (Tower)/132.4MHz (Approach)

Telephone: Lulsgate (027587) 4441

Owned by: Bristol Airport PLC

Cambridge (Teversham)

Opened on 8 October 1938, it replaced the smaller field situated a mile or so nearer to the town. It not only became the new home for the Cambridge and University Aero Clubs, but also for a training unit for RAF Reserve personnel. During the war well over 100 Tiger Moths were on the strength of 22 EFTS which operated alongside the Magisters, Masters and Austers of smaller specialised units. All aircraft were maintained by Marshalls, the airfield's owner.

Apart from looking after the local training aircraft, the company became involved in repair and overhaul work for the Air Ministry, particularly with Whitleys, Albemarles, Typhoons and Oxfords. Much work was also done on Mosquito modification and development including radar installation, deck landing conversions and target towing adaptations. The only operational sorties flown from Cambridge were those of Nos 2 and 16 Squadrons' Lysanders during the invasion scares of 1940.

After the war Cambridge reverted to civilian flying training using Tiger Moths, while the Marshall Rapides soon became familiar sights on charter work. RAF Reserve flying continued with 22RFS, Chipmunks replacing the Tiger Moths in 1950. Military contracts also flourished. Venom assembly and testing in the 1950s was followed by Canberra overhauls and modifications in the 1960s and 1970s. In 1966 Marshalls became the European centre for civil and military Hercules aircraft, which included the RAF fleet. Painting the latter was a specialised task and was carried out in a new hangar in which temperatures could be controlled. Originally intended to be long-lasting, the two-tone brown and black camouflage was replaced after a few years by green and grey. Yet another change of policy saw a third scheme devised which was of course good news for the paint manufacturers and Marshalls. The fuselage stretch modification to convert the type into a C Mk 3 was undertaken at Cambridge, the last of 29 aircraft being rolled out in November 1985. In 1982 Marshall was given the task of urgently converting some Hercules into tankers for the flight refuelling of similar aircraft. This work was completed in a remarkably short time allowing the type to play a significant role in the South Atlantic airbridge operations leading to the successful outcome of the Falklands campaign.

Lessons learned during the campaign convinced the Ministry of Defence that a large transport was needed for the dual purpose of troop carrier and flight refueller. After evaluating the KC-10A, a suitable type already in service with the USAF, costs were deemed too great. Six second-hand TriStar 500s were therefore bought from British Airways plus another three from Pan American. Marshall was awarded the contract to modify the machines for their new role. It was a long and by no means straightforward task, the first conversion taking almost two years to complete. Meanwhile the unconverted specimens served on the supply runs to the Falklands, awaiting their turn to be modified by the Cambridge company.

In 1990 Marshall won a £30 million contract to continue its maintenance support on the nine-strong RAF TriStar fleet over the next four years. Both major and minor inspections were included plus a non-programmed service in the event of unexpected technical faults. On the strength of the expertise gained during the 1980s, civilian specimens also appeared for overhaul, modification or repaint, British Airways was an early customer in 1986 when its TriStars began to receive interior refits and reskinning where necessary.

Since September 1987 a steady stream of BAe 146s have visited Cambridge for various work to be completed. This has included changing cabin configurations, installing galleys and other equipment specified by the operator, or carrying out the latest modifications.

A new type made its appearance at Cambridge in mid-July 1990 when the first of five MD-11s arrived for cabin and flightdeck fitting-out prior to delivery to American Airlines. At one stage in the late 1980s there were plans to build a new jumbo hangar to the north of the field. This was in anticipation of a contract to overhaul Boeing 747s, but when this did not materialise construction of the building was not started. With space already at a premium, it seems likely that some expedient will become necessary if the company is to cope with the growing wide-bodied business.

Marshall has also been a main service centre for Gulfstream aircraft for many years, examples of which are frequently to be seen wearing registrations and colours rare to the UK. Cessna Citations are also handled by the company.

Cambridge has never generated much airline traffic other than on holiday routes. In 1959 Pegasus Airlines offered an Ostend service for a time using Vikings, while Derby Airways introduced their seasonal Jersey operation. From 1964 onwards it became a part of the British Midland network, until in

1972 Air Anglia took over to operate in pool with Intra Airways. A brief attempt with a feeder service to Norwich was unsuccessful and in 1973 Intra assumed sole responsibility for the Jersey schedules. Dakotas were used for some years, but in 1976 Viscounts took over some of the timings, eventually replacing the older machines completely. The Heralds of Express Air Services supplemented the Viscounts in 1979.

The Channel Islands' licence changed hands once again in 1981, this time passing to Guernsey Airlines. This carrier was equipped with Short SD3-30s, but when later acquired by British Air Ferries the company added a Viscount to its fleet. In reality, aircraft from either company were then to be found operating the seasonal schedules, an arrangement which ended with the sale of Guernsey Airlines to Aurigny Air Services in October 1987. Dan-Air was contracted for the flights in 1988, with the charter work awarded to Air UK Leisure.

During the next two years the Channel Islands' links were handled by both Air UK and Brymon using BAe 146s and Dash Sevens respectively. Both were operated on a non-scheduled basis on Saturdays and Sundays.

Cambridge became the terminal for a regular weekday service at last when Suckling Airways took up residence in 1988 with its Dornier 228 after its enforced move from Ipswich. It was a far more suitable operating base for the aircraft although it did mean that the airline was no longer quite so conveniently placed for its previous customers. Nevertheless, the carrier overcame the problem and successfully continued its twice-daily sorties to Amsterdam and Manchester.

Resident at the airport are the Chipmunks of 5AEF, Bulldogs of the University Air Squadron, Cessnas of the Cambridge Aero Club, plus other club, company and privately owned machines.

Location and access: Situated 2 miles east of city and south of A1303 Newmarket Road. Car parking space. Access normally restricted to passengers and friends. A local Cambus route from the railway station or city centre serves the airport at frequent intervals taking about 15min for the journey. Other routes operate from Drummer Street bus station taking about 10min to reach the airport on their way to Newmarket
Terminal: Small but adequate for number of movements involved. Coffee bar

Spectator facilities: None provided. Around the perimeter there are good vantage points to be found which can be varied according to the position of the sun. Both landing and ground shots are possible, often with uncluttered backgrounds

Operators: Scheduled services by Suckling Airways (Dornier 228)

Charters and IT operators: Air UK (BAe 146, Boeing 737), Brymon Airways (Dash Seven/Eight). A number of airlines operate charters in conjunction with special events such as university conferences or classic horse races at nearby Newmarket. These include such as Anglo Cargo (One-Eleven), Transavia (Boeing 737), Braathens (Boeing 737), TAT (FH-227), KLM (Boeing 737), Air France (Boeing 727), Lufthansa (Boeing 737), Condor (Boeing 737), CTA (MD-87), Alisarda (MD-83), Trans European (Boeing 737). TEA UK (Boeing 737), TEA Basle (Boeing 737)

Movements (1989): Total 58,015 (air transport 2,525/club 28,115/military 22,190/private 3,659). Total passengers 25,389

Runways: 05/23 (6,446ft/1,965m) 02/20 (2,943ft/897m – grass) 13/31 (2,132ft/650m – grass) 05/23 (3,116ft/950m – grass)

Radio frequencies: 122.2MHz (Tower)/ 123.6MHz (Approach)

Telephone: Cambridge (0223) 61133

Owned and operated by: Marshall of Cambridge (Engineering) Ltd

Cardiff-Wales (Rhoose)

The decision to develop Rhoose was taken in 1952 when it became impractical to extend Cardiff's conveniently situated Pengam Moors airfield. The new airport became fully operational on 1 April 1954, after considerable alterations had been made to the buildings many of which were of wartime origin. Like many others, Rhoose was constructed for the RAF, becoming a base for Spitfire training, 53 OTU using it as a satellite for nearby Llandow from April 1942. This unit left after a year, a lengthy period of time passing before No 7 Air Gunnery School arrived in February 1944. This occupancy ended in August after which with the exception of a period as a bomb storage depot, the airfield was unused again until its transformation into a civil airport.

Rhoose immediately became the home of Cambrian Airways who in company with

Dan-Air and Aer Lingus, slowly expanded the scheduled services from the airport. ITs also began to play a significant part in the increasing traffic figures, until in the mid-1960s it was apparent that the old single storey buildings were becoming inadequate at peak times. An ambitious development programme resulted in the 1972 opening of the present modern terminal block, lengthened runway plus updated support services.

International movements were now possible on a larger scale and it was intended that the airport would handle the regional traffic for South Wales and South-west England. However, no progress has been made to fulfil the plans to serve the area across the Bristol Channel. A name change to Cardiff-Wales in 1978 helped to clarify its intended function, since its previous title of Glamorgan (Rhoose) had always proved rather confusing for overseas travellers.

The absorption of Cambrian into British Airways brought about a steady reduction in services through the airport, until in March 1980 all routes were relinquished. The engineering division continued to handle work on One-Eleven 400s for a time and Viscounts until March 1982 when the type was finally withdrawn from British Airways service. They remained a familiar sight at Cardiff however since their new owner, British Air Ferries, also took over the maintenance facility. This was not only to relieve their existing works at Southend, but also to acquire premises in which to design and produce a microlight aircraft. The first of these by Dragon Aircraft flew in the summer of 1982.

Both Dan-Air and Aer Lingus continued their association with Rhoose, although the latter's Dublin route was reduced to a single daily flight operated by British Airways in 1979. Air Wales set up its headquarters in 1977 to become the new locally based airline. However, the company ceased operations in 1979 after a take-over by Air Anglia (now Air UK).

As in the case at Bristol, when British Airways gave up the Cardiff routes, Dan-Air was awarded the licences. The airline already served the airport, subsequently becoming the sole operator of schedules. As a stop on the carrier's Link City network, Cardiff gained the attentions of Metropolitan Airways when it took over the operation in 1982, but with the company's demise in 1985 the cross-country route ceased to exist. Several attempts have been made to launch a service to Chester in the wake of

the defunct Air Wales, but none prospered.

Dan-Air's presence had been steadily reduced until its only contribution in 1990 was a Belfast schedule but even this was finally withdrawn in 1991. The company's Amsterdam operation was taken over by NetherLines in 1986 while Brown Air reintroduced the Leeds/Glasgow sectors in the following spring. The latter airline subsequently became Capital and as such introduced Jersey and Edinburgh links – the latter via Leeds northbound – but with the 360 making a transit stop at Bristol during its southbound travels. It was therefore something of a setback for the airport when Capital was forced to cease operations at the end of June 1990, thereby further reducing the range of the scheduled services available. It left Ryanair with the twice-weekday flights to Dublin and the two weekend sorties to Guernsey in the hands of Air UK.

Cardiff became the headquarters of Airways International Cymru when it started operations in early 1984 with a pair of One-Elevens. This carrier's declared policy was to concentrate on charters and to lease its small fleet out during the quieter winter months. The airline's career ended in January 1988 but it was replaced at the start of the summer season by newly-formed Amberair. An even shorter lifespan was experienced by this company before it was acquired by Bristol-based Paramount. In the meantime another 737-equipped charter company named Inter European Airways had been formed at Cardiff as a subsidiary of Aspro Travel. Thereafter the machines were to be found at all the familiar holiday airports, but in view of the declining IT market in 1990, the airline decided to diversify its activities. To achieve this aim a number of licence applications were submitted to the CAA covering a vast range of scheduled routes, many of them originating from Cardiff. If approved, it was hoped to launch the new venture during 1991, but a change of policy caused most requests to be withdrawn.

Long-haul charters have become a regular feature in recent years with transatlantic flights offered from the Welsh airport to the US and Canada throughout the season using TriStars, DC-8s and Boeing 767s of American Trans Air, Worldways and Britannia respectively.

Meanwhile, a steady programme of modernisation and expansion has been undertaken by the airport authorities including an enlarged passenger lounge area and office space for cargo agents in the terminal complex to mark the completion of the second stage of the five-year scheme.

After the departure of British Airways at the end of the 1970s, the maintenance area passed into the hands of British Air Ferries for a short time, essentially for the production of Dragon microlights. This project was soon abandoned bringing to an end the major engineering facility, a situation which was to last for serveral years. In the summer of 1990 it was announced that Cardiff had been chosen by British Airways as the future overhaul centre for its 747-400 fleet. One of the world's largest hangars capable of accepting four of the jets wingtip to wingtip will be built on the 29-hectare site. Work was due to commence in early 1991 so that the first aircraft can arrive for overhaul in 1993.

Local flying clubs operate a selection of light aircraft, while both private and company-owned machines are regular visitors. Rugby internationals, particularly those against France, generate a considerable volume of traffic from both UK and foreign airlines.

The Wales Aircraft Museum first opened at Rhoose in 1976 albeit on a small scale. It has been gradually expanded until now there are some two dozen aircraft displayed at a site on the approach road to the airport. Amongst the exhibits is the Viscount 802 G-AOJC which, although never a part of the Cambrian fleet, has been painted to represent the one-time local airline. Apart from the fuselage of another of the type (G-ANRS), the museum has otherwise concentrated its attention on acquiring military aircraft.

Location and access: Situated 12 miles southwest of Cardiff. Well signposted from the city and M4 Junction 33 via A4232 and A4050. Car park charges graduated. Airport Express bus service X51 operates hourly in both directions between the terminal and Cardiff Central bus and rail station Monday to Saturday, with reduced frequency on Sunday. It takes 30min to compete the journey

Terminal: Contains lounge, restaurant, bar, buffet and shop

Spectator facilities: Access to a good viewing terrace overlooking the apron can be gained either from the second floor of the terminal or via external stairs. Admission is free. All movements can be readily seen, while photographic opportunities vary with the stand used. Generally there are few problems but mornings are preferable in sunny conditions. A 135mm lens is useful but not essential

Operators: Scheduled services by Air France/Brit Air (Saab SF340), KLM CityHopper (Saab SF340, Fokker 50), Ryanair (ATR-42), Manx (Jetstream) *Charters and IT operators:* Adria Airways (Airbus A320), Air Columbus (Boeing 727), Air Europa (Boeing 737), American Trans Air (TriStar), Aviogenex (Boeing 727), Balkan (Tu-154), Britannia (Boeing 737/767), Cyprus Airways (Airbus A310), Inter European (Boeing 737), JAT (Boeing 737), Spanair (MD-83), Worldways (TriStar, DC-8).

Celtic Air and Jersey European operate post and small freight night flights

Movements (1989): Total 60,774 (air transport 10,299/club 35,766/private 9,302/test and training 3,621). Total passengers 735,715

Runways: 03/21 (3,670ft/1,119m), 12/30 (7,700ft/2,347m)

Radio frequencies: 125.0MHz (Tower), 125.85MHz (Approach)

Telephone: Rhoose (0446) 711111

Operated by: Cardiff-Wales Airport Ltd

Carlisle (Crosby)

Of wartime construction, the airfield was first used by the Hurricanes of 59 OTU in February 1941. Training of a different kind was commenced in August of the following year by 9 OTU of Coastal Command equipped with Whitleys and Beaufighters. The airfield became a part of Transport Command in August 1944, this time becoming the base of 109 OCU with its Dakotas. The unit later was renumbered 1383 TSCU still retaining the same type, remaining so until disbanded in May 1946. The airfield became unoccu-pied soon after and although the town of Carlisle was served almost every summer after scheduled services were reintroduced postwar, the airfield originally employed was RAF Silloth.

In the 1960s operations were moved to Crosby which was renovated and renamed Carlisle Airport. Control responsibility was in the hands of Casair Ltd, a company engaged in charter work and flying training. In 1967 Dan-Air restarted the traditional seasonal route to the Isle of Man, at first using Dakotas but in 1970 introducing Ambassadors. The service originated at

Top:
Aberdeen is the base of the appropriately titled airline which operates several schedules with leased 748s, in this case G-BFLL from Dan-Air. *AJW*

Above:
Birmingham European operates an increasing number of schedules from its home base with five One-Elevens, G-AVGP being one of the batch taxying past the excellent spectators' area. *AJW*

Below:
Janes Aviation now uses Trislander G-OJAV for freight services from Blackpool. *AJW*

Above:
Spain has produced a number of new airlines in recent years, one of the latest being Futura. Bournemouth was one of the UK airports regularly visited by 737-400 EC-ETB during the 1990 summer season. *AJW*

Below:
Seen departing on a Bristol-Amsterdam schedule, Saab 340B PH-KSB is resplendent in its new livery and KLM CityHopper titles following the merger of NLM and NetherLines. *AJW*

Bottom:
The RAF is not alone in sending its Hercules to Cambridge for attention, although the Moroccan military example CNA-OM was actually acting as a crew ferry for an ailing Gulfstream on this occasion. *AJW*

Newcastle, calling at Crosby en route. Two years later saw the operation sub-contracted to Kestrel for the season, while Dan-Air introduced a second route from the airport, this time to Jersey with BAe (HS) 748s.

In the meantime the Oxford based CSE company had taken over Casair and the airfield operation in July 1969. This resulted in a build up of flying training activities, but a cessation of charter work. The seasonal schedules continued, although Crosby became a terminal instead of merely a transit stop. In 1979, Intra took over the licence from Dan-Air in exchange for their Jersey-Staverton route. That summer the company employed a Viscount on the Jersey service, but due to the uncertainty of Carlisle's future, the airline moved the northern terminal to Prestwick for the 1980 season. By this time Jersey European had become the operator, again using a Viscount for the long haul south. Yet another reorganisation left JEA as a Bandeirante/Twin Otter operator, with the result that no Carlisle or Prestwick service was flown in 1981-82. Scheduled services did return to Carlisle however, when in March 1982 the airport became part of a short-lived bus stop type of operation flown by Air Ecosse to connect Liverpool, Blackpool, Barrow, Carlisle, Glasgow and Aberdeen with a twice weekly Twin Otter flight. During the summer of 1982, the airline served the Isle of Man, again with Twin

Otters. None of this was particularly profitable so not surprisingly the services were discontinued. Carlisle was not forsaken by the airline however, because it included the airport as a transit stop on a new route from Dundee to Heathrow in 1984. Using Short SD3-60s, load factors were not encouraging so the operation was taken over by Euroair in November 1985. While its 748s reversed the trend by providing a more comfortable trip for the passengers, nevertheless the service was withdrawn in early 1987 following a reorganisation within Euroair and the decision to discontinue its involvement with schedules. As a result the only regular flight from Carlisle became the seasonal once-weekly Viscount service to Jersey provided by British Air Ferries.

Fresh hopes were raised during the summer of 1987 for the revival of the London link which, when suspended, was just beginning to be fully appreciated by businessmen in particular. An application by Brymon to take over the licence was made to the CAA in the middle of the year, but instead the airline decided to concentrate its resources on the London City project with no further involvement in Carlisle. During 1988 Air Furness began regular links with the Isle of Man with an Islander and also proposed to introduce other routes. However, during the year the airline was forced to cease operations due to circumstances beyond its control, spelling an end to commercial flying at the Cumbrian airport for the time being. In early 1990 British Northern Airways announced its intention to operate schedules from Carlisle to Belfast, Dublin, Brussels and Heathrow. A request for a charter series to Jersey was later withdrawn. If successful in its applications, BNA expected to employ ATR-42s for the services, but no action could be taken before the CAA was satisfied with the financial state of the company.

Location and access: Situated 5 miles east-northeast of Carlisle off B6264 to Brampton. A local Ribble bus from the city bus station takes some 20min for the journey, but it then involves a walk of about one mile from the nearest alighting point

Terminal: Small building alongside the tower contains bar and buffet
Spectator facilities: Good viewing in the vicinity of the terminal which also provides a photographic vantage point. Landing shots are possible at the threshold of the runway in use
Operators: Scheduled services suspended. British Northern Airways (ATR-42) in prospect. A number of light aircraft are based at the airport
Movements (1989): Total 26,787 (air transport 353/club 8,147/test and training 14,380). Total passengers 2,182
Runways: 07/25 (6,026ft/1,837m)
01/19 (4,225ft/1,288m)
13/31 (2,982ft/909m used by helicopters only, except in emergencies)
Radio frequency: 123.6MHz (Tower and Approach)
Telephone: Crosby-on-Eden (0228-73) 641
Operated by: County Borough of Carlisle

Coventry (Baginton)

Unlike many of the municipalities that were struggling to provide a local airport in the 1930s, Coventry's authorities were able to benefit from the presence of an ambitious company already in residence on the outskirts of the city. Although Armstrong Whitworth possessed a small field from which it flew its lighter products, since the manufacturer was turning its attention towards a

bomber for the RAF, the idea of a larger facility nearby met with its approval. Work was already well advanced with a design to meet the requirements of the Air Ministry's specification B3/34, the first prototype flying in March 1936. By the time the second took to the air 11 months later, the Baginton factory had begun work. Taking the name of Whitley, progress with its production was slow and consequently the type was being overtaken by modern developments. At the

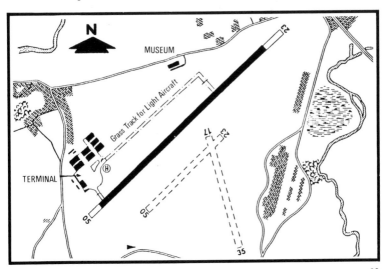

start of the war proposals were made that Armstrong Whitworth should produce the new twin-engined Manchester, but this and a similar scheme involving Halifaxes was abandoned in favour of later variants of the ageing Whitley. During the period from March 1937 to June 1943 the company delivered 1,812 examples of the type, most of them flying from Baginton.

From this point attention was turned to producing the radial-engined Lancaster II, although the airfield was also used for testing other versions of the bomber. Once the war in Europe was over, a contract was awarded to the manfacturer to bring the more plentiful Merlin-powered variant up to Far East standard. Lincolns were also included in this programme, a type built by Armstrong Whitworth between 1945 and 1948. Civil aviation was not forgotten, the company building an advanced flying wing intended for use as a mail carrier and the Apollo turboprop airliner. Prototypes of the latter were flown from Baginton but no production was forthcoming, the rival Viscount securing all orders.

Meanwhile links with Hawker Siddeley brought Meteor production to Coventry, while the design staff worked on various bomber and fighter projects. Although nothing came of most of these, the company's nightfighter development of the Meteor 7 was adopted by the RAF. Starting with the Mk 11, all of the aircraft destined for this role were built at Baginton as were indeed the Sapphire-powered Hunter 2s and 5s. Surprisingly, until October 1960 there was no hard runway at the airfield, most of the jet types flying from Bitteswell. It befell the Argosy to become the last machine to be constructed at Baginton, but this transport was only produced in small numbers before the factory closed on 16 July 1965.

Air transport movements had never been particularly numerous at Coventry although small carriers from time to time had introduced schedules to the Channel Islands and the Isle of Man. Provision of the runway was an improvement which was essential if the airport was to attract other airlines. It helped to encourage British United Air Ferries to start a car ferry service to Calais in 1964, an enterprise which lasted three years or so. A second attempt using the larger Carvair on a Channel Islands sector was launched in 1972, but this too only survived until the end of the following year. From this point until the early 1980s the sole operator of a scheduled passenger service was British

Midland with a seasonal operation to Jersey. There was an increase in the spring of 1982 when the resident company, Air Commuter, was awarded a licence for a Coventry-Paris link, the inaugural flight being made in May using a Bandeirante leased from Genair. The latter introduced its own schedules from Baginton on 5 April 1983, when the Short SD3-30s maintaining the Liverpool-Gatwick service began to call en route. In the meantime the Paris-bound passengers with Air Commuter were now travelling in a Jetstream contracted from Peregrine prior to delivery of the airline's own machine. Poor loads sadly brought a swift end to the Genair service on 13 August, although the company remained optimistic that it would return to Coventry in the future.

During May 1984 Air Commuter changed its name to Venture Airways, at the same time replacing its equipment with a HS 748 configured with a first class layout. Also appearing that summer were the newly acquired Viscount 700s of Janus Airways, the company which operated the air portion of Hards Travel's coach-air holidays to the Continent. Unfortunately this level of commercial activity was not to continue for very long. On 31 July it was announced that Venture Airways had suspended its Paris schedule, the last sortie by the 748 G-VAJK taking place on the previous day. In due course a liquidator was appointed thereby formally removing any chance of a resumption. Janus reverted to being an all-Herald operator during the following year, but a contraction of its type of business forced Hards to sell the carrier to Euroair in the spring of 1986. Charter flights by the latter frequented Coventry during the year, particularly on sectors to Eire. Applications were submitted to the CAA for scheduled licences to these destinations, but a change in company policy left the future of such operations in doubt. Nonetheless a scheduled service to Dublin was launched in 1989 but it was flown by a Ryanair One-Eleven. The limited programme proved sufficiently popular for the frequency to be increased to a daily service except Saturday in 1990, achieved by staging the Stansted flight via the Midlands airport. A Sunday service to Knock was also launched using an ATR-42. Air Transport Schiphol introduced another international route when it began a twice-weekday link with Eindhoven in the Netherlands.

For many years the seasonal summer trips to the Channel Islands almost became a tradition. Both British Midland and British Air Ferries operated the flights, the latter employing Viscounts for its charter services. Eventually BMA was alone on the route for several seasons, until in 1990 it also removed the sector from its network.

Coventry became the main base of Air Atlantique early in 1986, its DC-3 fleet and Bristol Freighter moving in from Stansted. Thereafter freight charters kept the machines busy, while passenger pleasure flights continued to be popular. In the early part of 1987 the airport became the base for a pair of DC-6s acquired by the company for longer range cargo work.

General aviation is also well catered for with several operators and maintenance companies in residence. A change of airport operator was planned during 1982, but after much deliberation the City Council continued in the role. At last there were signs that it wished to develop the airport rather than close it. Modest extensions to the terminal were completed by the summer of 1985, going a long way to easing the congestion particularly at times of diversions or charters using larger aircraft.

Also located at Coventry is the Midland Air Museum, which contains amongst its growing number of interesting exhibits the locally-built Argosy G-APRL. Operated by Air Bridge for Elan International, the aircraft was delivered to its birthplace on 20 February 1987 to begin its retirement alongside the new 10,000sq ft 'Sir Frank Whittle Jet Heritage Centre' which eventually is intended to house most of the collection.

Location and access: Situated 3 miles south of Coventry off A45. Car park charged on a pay and display basis. Midland Red provides a bus route which links Coventry (Pool Meadow bus station) with Leamington via the airport access road taking some 15min for the journey from the city

Terminal: Single storey building containing lounge area. Vending machines are available for drinks

Spectator facilities: None provided. Photography and viewing possible from the short-term car park area and vantage points on airfield perimeter

Operators: Scheduled services by Ryanair (One-Eleven, ATR-42), Air Transport Schiphol (Cheyenne)

Charter operators: British Air Ferries (Viscount), Air Atlantique (DC-3, DC-6). Other charters are handled from time to time, particularly when there are special events in progress locally. There are a number of private and club aircraft based at the airport

Movements (1989): Total 70,078 (air transport 1,623/club 11,305/private 19,419/test and training 33,641). Total passengers 18,288

Runways: 05/23 (5,300ft/1,615m) 05/23 (1,690ft/515m – grass) 17/35 (2,673ft/815m – grass)

Radio frequencies: 119.25MHz (Tower/ Approach)/122.0MHz (Radar)

Telephone: Coventry (0203) 301717

Operated by: Coventry District Council

Dundee (Riverside)

As the name suggests, this small airport occupies a narrow strip of land between the Tay and the main road. It was opened in 1963 on the site of former playing fields. Scheduled services from Dundee started after a couple of years or so when Strathair received approval for a Dundee-Edinburgh route, later expanded to take in Prestwick and Inverness. The sector serving Prestwick was started in July 1966 and was intended to act as a feeder for international flights. It did not receive much support however, which meant that after two months the service was withdrawn.

Also in July another route was introduced, this time to Glasgow with British Eagle employing a Dove. Again the idea was to connect with the carrier's London trunk ser-

vices. The airline carried on for almost two years, but when Autair began a Dundee-London operation, inevitably support quickly disappeared and with it the link with Glasgow.

Although Autair had attempted to use Riverside, the field suffered from waterlogging making the use of 748s or Heralds impractical. As a result and two years of negotiations later, the airline received permission to use RAF Leuchars as the Dundee terminal, commencing in April 1968. The enterprise was again short lived since the following year Autair abandoned all scheduled work when it became involved entirely with ITs as Court Line.

After an inactive period, the airport came to life again in 1971 when the Glasgow route was reopened, this time by Loganair using an Islander. Although subsidised by

Dundee Corporation, the airline could not absorb the increasing losses resulting in the link once again being severed, this time in May 1975.

Throughout its life as an airport, Riverside had been an all grass field. Following a decision taken in 1977, a tarmac runway was provided which has allowed more reliable operations. Schedules subsequently returned to Dundee with Air Ecosse offering Manchester and Aberdeen services, followed in 1984 by a London link after many years. Using Short SD3-60s, two return trips were made each weekday via Carlisle, the timings such that a day trip to the capital was practical. However, the airline found difficulty in bringing the route into profitability, so in November 1985 Euroair took over the service. Immediately there was an improvement in the loads carried, probably due to the greater comfort offered by the BAe 748 employed. However, a change of policy in early 1987 resulted in the carrier withdrawing from the scheduled scene although it continued to operate the services to Manchester and Aberdeen on behalf of Air Ecosse throughout the latter's period of reorganisation.

During the year Euroair's Scottish operations were taken over by Business Air, a new airline formed at Aberdeen for the purpose. A service between Dundee and Esbjerg was inaugurated in the spring of 1988 while the regular sorties to Aberdeen and Manchester continued with Bandierantes. Traffic was encouraging and by 1990 the company was actively considering the acquisition of a larger type. This was achieved during the year when the Swiss regional carrier Crossair transferred a Saab SF340 after taking a financial interest in the Scottish airline. Applications were also made to the CAA for several new routes including Birmingham, Liverpool, Edinburgh, Manchester and East Midlands. There has been no further interest shown in the dormant Heathrow sector although in 1987 Brymon had been expected to start the service with a leased BAe 748. However, after a change of policy the airline dropped the scheme.

Location and access: Situated 2 miles west of the city centre between the north bank of the Firth of Tay and the A85.

Terminal: Small single storey building containing waiting area. Drinks machine provided

Spectator facilities: None provided. Views of the apron can be obtained from the east side of the terminal, but due to the growth of the shrubbery this vantage point is becoming less useful. Photography is possible through the perimeter fence to the west and all movements can be readily observed

Operator: Business Air (Bandeirante, Short SD3-60, Saab SF340)

Movements (1989): Total 34,357 (air transport 2,409/club 27.411/private 1,732). Total passengers 11,270
Runway: 10/28 (3,608ft/1,100m)

Radio frequency: 122.9MHz (Tower and Approach)
Telephone: Dundee (0382) 643242
Operated by: Tayside Regional Council

East Midlands (Castle Donington)

Castle Donington was destined to become the satellite airfield for Wymeswold, opening as such on 1 January 1943. Accordingly part of 28 OTU was transferred to the new station, using its Wellingtons for the urgent task of aircrew training. A few Lysanders and Martinets were also on strength for target towing purposes, later replaced by Hurricanes. The first crews passed out in June 1943, making sorties over enemy territory at the end of the training courses prior to joining front line squadrons.

In October 1944, the unit was disbanded, but Castle Donington then became host to 108 OTU, sharing its Dakotas with the parent airfield at Wymeswold. The output target was 24 crews every three weeks from courses of 12 weeks duration, resulting in a considerable build up of flying hours at the bases.

With the war in Europe over, the unit was renumbered 1382 Transport Conversion Unit on 10 August 1945, but retaining the same aircraft. By this time, Transport Command was busy ferrying supplies and per-sonnel to and from the Far and Middle East areas, a task in which Castle Donington's Dakotas also became involved. However by September 1946, the much reduced aircrew requirement meant that the airfield was no longer required and therefore it was closed down.

In the 1950s it was realised that the exist-ing airport at Burnaston had limited develop-ment potential. Serious thought was given to find a successor, the eventual choice being the long abandoned Castle Donington. Although employing the old site, very little proved of use during the conversion. Even the original main runway had to be com-pletely relaid, as did the various taxiways and most of the internal roads. When it was opened in April 1965, East Midlands became the first new municipal airport to have been constructed in Britain since the war. Soon afterwards British Midland opened its operating base to become the first resident airline. The airport was also chosen as the base of the Argosy and Mer-chantman equipped airline Air Bridge Carri-ers, while in 1980 the newly formed IT car-rier Orion Airways began its commercial career. Scheduled services were also intro-duced by Alidair, a company which began charter operations from East Midlands in 1972, later trading as Inter City Airlines until its demise in August 1983.

While British Midland still provides the majority of the schedules from the airport, other companies have joined it from time to time through the years. NetherLines introduced an Amsterdam sector, while Air Ecosse was successful in acquiring the Scottish licences previously held by Inter City. However, it was not long before difficulties led to these domestic routes being flown by Peregrine Air Services on behalf of the holder. Eventually the latter carrier, under its new name of Aberdeen Airways, was awarded the licences in its own right. After several years' absence a Dublin route was reinstated in the mid-1980s, this time using the Short SD3-60s of Aer Lingus. Although starting life exclusively as a charter airline, in 1986 Orion successfully gained permission to fly schedules from East Midlands to Palma and Malaga, both destinations already frequently visited during the course of its IT work.

The airline had quickly won a reputation for its quality of service, so when the news was released that Orion was to be integrated into Britannia during 1989, it came as a surprise to the industry and public alike. It was not long before the familiar livery and titles disappeared from aircraft and buildings at East Midlands because the new owner understandably intended to concentrate its activities at its Luton base. Naturally the scheduled licences were transferred to Britannia without interruption, but at the end of the 1990 summer season the airline decided to withdraw from this market in favour of its charter work.

Field Aircraft has also been a resident of East Midlands for many years. Nowadays the company is responsible for the installation of flightdeck instrumentation, avionics, wiring, passenger cabin interiors and final painting of Jetstreams that arrive from Prestwick in basic form. The completion programme takes 20 days on average before the aircraft are flown back to their birthplace in readiness for delivery to the customers. By October 1990 Fields had handled 300 Jetstreams since the company became associated with the type in 1982. From 1991 the East Midlands facility will be involved in the same way with the new Series 41, but in this case the manufacturer intends to complete the aircraft on the Prestwick production line rather than fly the aircraft to Fields.

From the time that its operational life began, the airport has developed into an important centre, serving not only neighbouring Derby and Nottingham, but many other towns thanks to its very convenient position just off the M1 motorway.

Recognising the potential, the authorities commenced a major expansion programme in 1981 to give additional cargo facilities together with a large apron extension. Once completed the attention was turned to the passenger terminal with the result that a much improved building became available to handle the growing traffic. A western taxiway was also laid to eliminate the need for back-tracking along the runway.

As the airport grew so the valuable space occupied by the spectators' enclosure and the Loughborough and Leicester Aircraft Museum was needed. This could easily have meant the end of the excellent viewing arrangements enjoyed for some years, but instead the authorities agreed to provide an Aeropark to combine both the facility for observing the airport movements with static exhibits and an exhibition hall. Completed in 1984, the enterprise has proved very successful and has a Varsity, Vulcan, S-55, the SA-1 Sheriff and an Argosy within the compound.

Location and access: Situated 2 miles from M1 Junction 24 via A453. Ample parking space, graduated charges. Various local bus services connect the airport with Derby (12 miles), Nottingham (14 miles) and Leicester (20 miles). From the airport terminal bus stop it is about a 10min walk to the signposted Aeropark

Terminal: A modern two-storey building containing a buffet on the ground floor, plus a choice of eating styles within two areas on the first floor. There are two bars in the public section plus a shop with a good selection of aviation books

Spectator facilities: For short-term viewing there is a balcony along the front of the first floor providing excellent opportunities for apron shots. Admission free. At the eastern end of the airport is located the Aeropark reached from a point near the airport entrance. There is a fixed entrance fee for a car which includes all occupants. From the grass covered mounds excellent viewing is possible while photographs of aircraft on the adjacent taxiway or landing on runway 27 can be obtained, although a 200mm or zoom lens is necessary

Operators: Scheduled services by British

Midland (DC-9, BAe ATP, Boeing 737), Aer Lingus (Short SD3-60, Fokker 50), Aberdeen Airways (BAe 748, Gulfstream 1), Air Bridge/Elan (Merchantman, Electra-cargo). A number of other freight flights are made in the late evening or early morning by operators of Bandeirantes, Twin Otters, Dornier 228s, Super King Airs, Short SD3-30/3-60s, Heralds, Titans and Navajos during the course of mail or parcel work *Charter and IT operators:* Adria Airways (DC-9), Air Atlantis (Boeing 737), Air Europa (Boeing 737), Air Malta (Boeing 737), Airtours (MD-83), Air UK Leisure (Boeing 737), Aviogenex (Boeing 727/737), Dan-Air (Boeing 727/737), Britannia (Boeing 737/767), JAT (Boeing 727, DC-9), Spanair (MD-83), TEA (UK) (Boeing 737), Viva Air (Boeing 737).

Other movements are created by the numerous company operated, club and privately owned aircraft based at the airport. It is also used as an alternative in bad weather conditions for Birmingham, Luton, Norwich and Leeds

Movements (1989): Total 74,267 (air transport 29,947/club 29,014/private 9,799). Total passengers 1,453,985
Runway: 09/27 (7,480ft/2.280m)
Radio frequencies: 124.0MHz (Tower)/ 119.65MHz (Approach)
Telephone: Derby (0332) 810621
Owned and operated by: East Midlands International Airport PLC

Edinburgh (Turnhouse)

Turnhouse opened in 1915, becoming the most northerly of the defence stations in World War I. Between the wars it became the home of No 603 (City of Edinburgh) Squadron, for the majority of its peacetime existence equipped in turn with DH-9As, Westland Wapitis, Hawker Harts and Hind light bombers. A change of role found the squadron with Spitfires at the outbreak of war, the airfield at the same time coming under the control of Fighter Command. Hard runways were laid permitting it to be used on a regular basis by squadrons resident for varying periods of time.

Although scheduled passenger services began in 1947, it was some years before traffic built up. By the mid-fifties Viscounts began to replace the Pionairs on the main routes, at the same time offering a modest increase in frequencies. A brand new terminal was opened in 1956, which received a further extension five years later. The midsixties saw Comets employed on a few prestige flights to counter the growing competition, but the remainder of the timings were maintained by Vanguards and Viscounts.

It became apparent by the late sixties that major development was necessary if Turnhouse was to cope with the increasing traffic created by the oil business. The BAA assumed control in April 1971, shortly afterwards launching a programme to provide a new runway and terminal building.

British Airways was therefore able to introduce a shuttle service to London in 1976 using Tridents without restriction. The following year saw the completion of the terminal designed to cope with 1,500,000 passengers each year. International routes available dwindled in the early 1980s until only Amsterdam and Dublin were served non-stop, but gradually new destinations in Germany were added by BA while Air France returned to the airport with a Paris link. There is a reasonable choice of domestic services on offer, the most significant addition coming with the award of a licence to British Midland enabling the carrier to operate to Heathrow in competition with the British Airways shuttle.

For many years British Caledonian operated a regular schedule to Gatwick, but with the takeover by BA, the licence was duly awarded to Air UK. Marketed as the Sterling service, the company introduced the BAe 146 to the route in October 1988 and was rewarded with traffic figures considerably better than those experienced by the previous operator. Edinburgh was also served by Chieftain Airways during its short career in 1987; a duty taken over by Scottish European in November 1988 when it began serving Brussels and Frankfurt. Activities continued into 1990 but the company was then forced to suspend its operations pending a possible reorganisation

Frequent use is made of the airport by military aircraft as well as foreign charter, company and privately owned machines.

Location and access: Situated 8 miles west of Edinburgh, reached via signposted access on A8 midway between the Maybury and Newbridge roundabouts. Car park charges graduated. Lothian Regional Transport provides a link with the city centre at Waverley about every 30min. Journey time is approximately 25min

Terminal: Contains large buffet, bar, restaurant, shop and lounge area

Spectator facilities: A gallery is provided along the front of the second floor of the terminal, admission free. Overlooking the apron and runway, it provides good opportunities for both viewing and photography although a telephoto lens is desirable for most shots. Facing north, there is no problem with the sun should it be in evidence. Access is signposted via internal stairs and an internal observation area which is useful in times of inclement weather. Other vantage points exist near the runway thresholds and the old terminal building, now used as a cargo centre

Operators: Scheduled services by Aberdeen Airways (Gulfstream 1, BAe 748), Aer Lingus (Fokker 50), Air France (Fellowship, Boeing 737), Air UK (Friendship, BAe 146), British Airways (Boeing 757, BAe 748, One-Eleven), British Midland (Boeing 737), Brymon Airways (Dash Eight), Loganair (Short SD3-60, BAe 146/ATP, Twin Otter), Sabena/Delta Air Transport (Fellowship, BAe 146)

Charter and IT operators: Adria Airways (DC-9), Air Atlantis (Boeing 737), Air Europa (Boeing 737/757), Air Malta (Boeing 737), Air 2000 (Boeing 757), ATI (DC-9), Aviogenex (Boeing 727/737), Britannia (Boeing 737), British Midland (Boeing 737), Cyprus Airways (Airbus A310), Lineas Aéreas Canarias (MD-83), Norjet (Boeing 737), Worldways (TriStar).

Mail and parcels traffic brings a variety of smaller types into the airport during the night. There are also a number of company, club and privately owned aircraft based at Edinburgh

Movements (1989): Total 103,104 (air transport 46,931/club 29,014/private 8,019/military 15,360). Total passengers 2,460,033

Runways: 07/25 (8,400ft/2,560m) 13/31 (6,000ft/1,829m) 08/26 (2,982ft/909m)

Radio frequencies: 118.7MHz (Tower)/ 121.2MHz (Approach)

Telephone: Edinburgh (031) 333 1000

Operated by: Edinburgh Airport Ltd

Exeter (Clyst Honiton)

Officially opened on 30 June 1938, although both Jersey Airways and Railway Air Services had included Exeter in their route network from mid-1937. A Bristol-Plymouth-Land's End-Scilly Islands service was routed via Exeter by Great Western & Southern Airlines from May 1939, but at the outbreak of war these civil flights were suspended. The airfield handled various miscellaneous units until it became an official RAF station on 6 July 1940. Thereafter fighter squadrons came and went, Nos 87 and 213 serving during the Battle of Britain.

In April 1944 the airfield assumed the identity of Station 463 for the benefit of the USAAF. The 440th Troop Carrier Group arrived with its C-47s in readiness for the D-Day activities and subsequent sorties over Normandy. By August the war had moved on, leaving Exeter to receive the Masters and Hotspurs of 3 Glider Training School. This unit remained until August 1945, its place taken for short periods by operational squadrons including the Meteors of No 222 Squadron.

The Ministry of Civil Aviation took over control of the airfield on 1 January 1947, although military aircraft were to be seen for a long time to come. The Tiger Moths and Chipmunks of 10 Reserve Flying School remained until disbanded in 1954, while 3 Civil Anti-Aircraft Co-operation Unit used a variety of aircraft types during its long existence at Exeter.

In 1952 Jersey Airlines reintroduced the Channel Islands routes, which still remain popular today albeit with different carriers. A London link was attempted briefly by Olley Air Services about the same period, followed later by services to Gatwick, Newquay, Plymouth and the Scillies flown for a time by British Westpoint. In the late 1950s/early 1960s both Starways and North-South Airlines connected Exeter to the north, while South West Aviation came on the scene much later with a Cherbourg service in 1970.

The demise of all these airlines in some cases saw the end of the routes, in others the licences were taken over by the next ambitious carrier. British Island Airways and Brymon Airways provided the services during most of the 1970s to such places as Belfast, Channel Islands, Dublin and the Scillies. The pair were joined in 1978 by Air Westward, which began by operating Titans to Amsterdam, Gatwick, Glasgow, Paris and later Brussels. The company did not survive very long, with the result that BIA took over the ailing airline after 10 months or so, operating it under the name BIA-Air West. By October 1979 it was common knowledge that BIA and Air Anglia plus associated carriers were to merge to form Air UK. Exeter became the headquarters of the combined six-strong Bandeirante fleet, the type then used on routes requiring less capacity. In March 1981 this group became the Air UK Commuter Services division, operating a pruned network at frequencies likely to attract businessmen in particular. Gradually Exeter saw the routes on offer contract, until by the summer of 1982 only a daily Jersey service and a weekday Gatwick/Rotterdam through flight was available in the Air UK network. Brymon continued to serve the airport throughout the decade with its Twin Otters connecting Exeter with Plymouth and London (Gatwick), until in 1989 most flights were upgraded to the Dash Seven. However, one of the smaller machines was retained because until the runway at St Marys is lengthened, the airline is restricted to using the type for the Isles of Scilly services. The operation finally ended at the conclusion of the 1990 summer season when Brymon disposed of its Twin Otter. Later the carrier applied for the Channel Islands' licences vacated by Air UK, but at the same time suspended its Gatwick service due to rising costs.

As Jersey European expanded, it chose the Devon airport for its administration centre in January 1986, although this did not mean any less commitment to the Channel Islands. Two routes were added to the network, namely those to Belfast and Dublin — both one-time Air UK territory, but now intended as a means of feeding Irish traffic to Jersey and Guernsey - destinations regularly served by JEA. In the event the route to the Republic was later dropped, but a twice-daily link with Manchester has proved very successful.

Westcountry Aircraft Servicing carries out regular maintenance and overhaul work on piston and turboprop airliners belonging to various carriers. The airport also frequently serves as a haven for migrating Shorts SD3-30s and 3-60s. A number of these types are often to be seen displaying evidence of past operators as they await the call for renewed action. The operation of school, club, private and company owned aircraft contributes to the movements.

Plans have been drawn up for the development of a new cargo centre and better access to the main road. In the past there was a minimal amount of cargo handled at Exeter, but with the realisation that it can significantly affect the prosperity of regional airports, a greater effort is to be made to attract more business.

Location and access: Situated 4 miles east of Exeter, 1½ miles from M5 Junction 29. Turn off A30 at Clyst Honiton towards Farringdon and Aylesbere. Car park has graduated charges with no free period. The Rainbow Bus Company runs a service from Exeter coach and St David's rail stations three times each weekday and once on Saturday. Devon General routes 60, 60A and 60B to Clyst Honiton run at hourly intervals from Exeter bus station. This method involves a walk of about one mile to the terminal, or ¾-mile to a good vantage point.

Terminal: Includes a lounge, licensed bar, buffet, shop and conference room.

Spectator facilities: A good viewing balcony is provided on the first floor with access from within the terminal. It offers good photographic opportunities for apron and runway shots, the latter requiring a 200mm lens. The small layby situated along the approach road has now been closed to ensure clear access in the event of an emergency but, if on foot, photography is still possible. As an alternative the long-stay car park now extends alongside the taxiway

Operators: Scheduled services by Brymon (Dash Seven), Jersey European (Friendship)

Charter and IT operators: Adria Airways (DC-9), Air Europe (Boeing 737), Air Malta (Boeing 737), Aviogenex (Boeing 737), Cyprus Airways (Airbus A320), Lineas Aéreas Canarias (MD-83), Spanair (MD-83), Worldways (DC-8), J & J Aviation (Bandeirante)

Movements (1989): Total 56,462 (air transport 9,728/club 22,335, private 13,313). Total passengers 237,942

Runways: 08/26 (6,840ft/2,083m), 13/31 (4,393ft/1,339m)

Radio frequencies: 119.8MHz (Tower)/ 128.15MHz (Approach)

Telephone: Exeter (0392) 67433

Operated by: Exeter Airport Ltd

Gatwick

Although licensed for flying in 1930, Gatwick did not officially become an airport until June 1936. During the intervening years it became very popular with jockeys and the more influential racegoers because of its close proximity to the race course. Nevertheless, the airfield did little to reward its owners, causing it to change hands four times in almost as many years. By the mid-1930s the projected airport was under development, one of its design features being a very advanced terminal building which, because of its appearance, became known as the 'Beehive'. It incorporated an underground passageway to the adjacent railway station, again a novel feature in 1936 and an idea which 50 years later has been adopted by very few authorities. Gatwick was equipped with night flying aids and two hangars were constructed for the benefit of the expected operators. One of these was British Airways, an airline formed on 1 October 1935 by the merger of Spartan Airways, United Airways and Hillman Airways, the last named being the successful private company based at Stapleford, Essex. Unfortunately its new home suffered from waterlogging, a problem which resulted in the newcomer moving out after one year's residence.

A growing need for military personnel was responsible for the arrival of No 19 E&RFTS complete with Tiger Moths and Harts in October 1937. Additional buildings were then necessary especially since the unit was enlarged in the following year with a number of Magisters. At the beginning of the war the school was closed down and civil flying ended. Blenheim squadrons were the main occupants of Gatwick until September 1940 when the station came under the wing of Army Co-Operation Command. Lysanders then became a familiar sight, outstaying the unsuccessful Tomahawk intended as its

replacement. Mustangs took over in early 1942, taking part in several operations including the ill-fated Dieppe landings in August. With the formation of the Tactical Air Force in mid-1943, the Army Co-Operation Command was absorbed into it leaving Gatwick to be taken over by No 11 Group. Numerous Spitfire units passed through during the winter of 1943/44, flying on escort and attack missions. At the time of the D-Day landings much importance was placed on the activities of the photo-reconnaissance Mustang squadrons which had arrived just prior to the invasion. By August the operational units had moved out, their place taken by those involved in communications and support. Gradually Gatwick was run down as the size of the RAF shrunk after the end of the war; the military finally relinquished its control on 31 August 1946.

As was customary in those days it was the Ministry of Civil Aviation that became responsible for the airfield. Despite its active role during the six hectic years no hard runways had been provided, a fact which did little to attract civilian operators. Nonetheless, a number of companies took up residence in the period up to 1956, engaging in both charter and maintenance work. Already plans were being laid for Gatwick to become London's second airport, necessitating the dispersal of all occupants while its reconstruction was underway. When opened two years later it possessed a single 7,000ft

(2,133m) runway and a large apron over which a pier stretched from the brand-new terminal building. As before, this was connected to the railway, with British Rail rebuilding its station adjacent to the airport complex. On 9 June 1958 the opening ceremony was performed by The Queen and Prince Philip, the couple arriving in a Heron of the Royal Flight.

The formation of British United Airways in 1960 brought a considerable increase in activity at Gatwick, both scheduled and charter. A rapid upsurge of ITs in the 1960s saw a constant stream of airliners using the facilities, which by this time had been expanded to include two additional piers. To accommodate the larger types then coming into service, the runway was extended, first to 8,200ft (2,499m) in 1964 and later to 10,000ft (3,048m). Another major development began in the mid-1970s involving a vast terminal extension, multi-storey car park and a direct access road to the M23 motorway. Airside changes included additional parking areas and taxiways, while an emergency runway was laid parallel to the existing strip with completion in October 1985. Unfortunately the separation distance was insufficient to permit its use for regular traffic.

Always a popular airport with the IT carriers, those offering scheduled services have also steadily grown in number. Home of British Caledonian, this operator made a considerable contribution to the movement statistics with both domestic, European and intercontinental flights until becoming a part of British Airways at the end of 1987. Dan-Air likewise is engaged in both types of operation, while the larger US airlines began to expand their networks to use Gatwick as the UK gateway in the 1980s. Such was the growth that plans were submitted for a second terminal on the north side of the airport. Connected to the original building by a transit system, the new complex opened in March 1988.

Location and access: Situated 28 miles south of London on the A23 with a direct link to the M23 at Junction 9. Multi-storey and open car parks with graduated charges provided for both terminals. By rail the Gatwick Express runs nonstop between Victoria and the airport every 15min during the day, journey time 30min. On Sundays the trip takes 35min and during the night the trains run hourly with an elapsed time of up to 45min. Two Gatwick Link trains run every hour between the airport and London Bridge with a journey time of 35min. Speedlink coaches connect Gatwick with Heathrow every 20min during the morning, half-hourly in the afternoon with an hourly service in the evening. The trip takes about 60min depending of traffic congestion on the M25. Service 777 runs to Victoria coach station, while the 747 routes to Heathrow and Luton airports. Further details from London Country on 0293-502116. There are frequent local buses to both Crawley and Horley on routes C1, C2, 405, 422, and 773. Express coaches link various parts of the country with the London airports

Terminal: The large south building contains restaurants and snack bars on the catering level above the International arrivals hall. Shops and banks are also available. Similar facilities are provided in the north terminal

Spectator facilities: A gallery is situated on the roof of the south terminal building giving good views of all movements, although some are rather distant. There is an admission charge. A refreshment buffet is available. As a photographic vantage point it has its limitations although it is possible to secure shots of aircraft using the satellite and some of the nearer stands. This restriction is a pity since Gatwick does handle airlines not to be seen elsewhere in the UK. The provision of a TV monitor for checking arrivals and departures is to be applauded. There are no facilities provided in the north terminal, neither is it possible to view through windows on the landside

Operators: Scheduled services by Adria Airways (MD-80), Aer Lingus (Boeing 737), Aero Lloyd (DC-9), Aigle Azur (Bandeirante), Air France (Boeing 727/737, Airbus A320), Air Gambia (DC-8), Air Lanka (TriStar), Air Malta (Boeing 737, Airbus A320), Air New Zealand (Boeing 747), Air Seychelles (Boeing 767), Air UK (BAe 146), Air Vendee (Dornier 228), Air Zimbabwe (Boeing 707/767), All Nippon Airways (Boeing 747), American Airlines (DC-10), ATI (DC-9), Avianca (Boeing 747), Brit Air (Bandeirante, SF340, ATR-42), British Airways (Boeing 737/747/757, One-Eleven, TriStar, Airbus A320, DC-10), Brymon Airways (Dash Seven), CAAC (Boeing 747SP), Cameroon Airlines (Boeing 747), Canadian Airlines International (Boeing 767), Cathay Pacific (Boeing 747), Contactair (Jetstream), Continental Airlines (Boeing 747, DC-10), Cyprus Airways (Airbus A310), Dan-Air (One-Eleven, BAe 146, Boeing 737), Delta (TriStar), Emirates

(Airbus A310), Garuda International (Boeing 747), GB Air (Boeing 737), Hamburg Airlines (Dash Eight, Fokker 100), Iberia (Boeing 727, DC-9, MD-87), JAT (Boeing 737, DC-9), KLM CityHopper (Fokker 50), Korean Air (Boeing 747), Lucas Air Transport (Bandeirante, Beech 200), Lufthansa (Boeing 737), Maersk (Boeing 737), Noble Air (Boeing 727), Northwest Airlines (Boeing 747, DC-10), Philippine Airlines (Boeing 747), RFG (ATR-42), Royal Nepal Airlines (Boeing 757), Sabena (Boeing 747), SAS (DC-9), Transavia (Boeing 737), Transwede (Boeing 737, MD-80), TWA (Boeing 767, TriStar), Uganda Airlines (DC-10), USAir (Boeing 767), Virgin Atlantic (Boeing 747), Yemen Airways (Boeing 727), ZAS (MD-80)

Charter and IT operators: Aeroflot (Tu-134/154, Il-76), Adria Airways (DC-9), Air Atlantis (Boeing 737), Air Canada (TriStar), Air City (Caravelle), Air Columbus (Boeing 727), Air Europa (Boeing 737/757), Air Malta (Boeing 737, Airbus A320), Air UK Leisure (Boeing 737), Air 2000 (Boeing 757), Alitalia (MD-80), American Trans Air (TriStar, Boeing 757), ATI (DC-9),

Aviogenex (Boeing 727/737), Balair (DC-9), Balkan (Tu-154), Britannia Airways (Boeing 737/757/767), Caledonian Airways (Boeing 757, TriStar), Canadian Airlines International (Boeing 767), CTA (MD-80), Dan-Air (Boeing 727/737, One-Eleven), El Al (Boeing 707), Futura Airways (Boeing 737), Kar-Air (DC-9, Airbus A300), Lineas Aéreas Canarias (MD-80), LOT (Tu-134), Monarch Airlines (Boeing 737/757/767, Airbus A300), Nationair (DC-8, Boeing 747/757), Royal Air Maroc (Boeing 737), Tarom (IL-18, Tu-154), TEA (Boeing 737), Transwede (MD-80), Worldways (DC-8, Boeing 737, TriStar)

Movements (1989): Total 205,395 (air transport 190,877/private 2,206/positioning 11,676). Total passengers 21,258,486

Runways: 08R/26L (10,363ft/3,159m), 08L/26R (8,415ft/2,565m used only in emergencies or if 08R/26L is closed, otherwise it serves as a taxiway)

Radio frequencies: 124.225MHz (Tower)/ 125.875MHz (Approach)/ 119.6MHz (Radar)

Telephone: (0293) 28822 or 081-668 4211

Operated by: Gatwick Airport Ltd

Glasgow (Abbotsinch)

The airfield was established in 1932 for the RAF, becoming the home of 602 (City of Glasgow) Squadron. Initially a light bomber unit equipped with Westland Wapitis, Hawker Hinds, Harts and later Hectors, its role changed during 1938 to that of a fighter squadron, receiving Spitfire Is by September 1939. The airfield remained under RAF control during the first three years of war, until in 1943 it was transferred to the Fleet Air Arm. As a Royal Naval Air Station it took the name of HMS *Sanderling*, remaining operational until the end of October 1963. Much of its activities involved the overhaul and repair of aircraft attached to carrier based squadrons, its close proximity to Glasgow docks making it ideal for this purpose.

After its closure, the airfield was prepared for use as a civil airport under Glasgow Corporation's control, finally taking over from Renfrew in May 1966. The modern facilities were vastly superior to those of its overcrowded predecessor, immediately encouraging new airlines to include it in their route networks. It followed that during its first 10 operational years, passenger numbers and aircraft movements increased to such an extent that major surgery to the terminal became necessary. Under British Airports

Authority since 1975, it was expected that the new extensions planned would cope with the annual figure of 3.5 million passengers forecast for the late 1980s.

One of the major highlights of 1975 was the start of the UK's first Shuttle service, operated by British Airways with Tridents between Glasgow and Heathrow. Nowadays the Boeing 757 has taken over the duties. The airport is in fact well served by airlines with a good choice of scheduled and IT flights available both domestic and international. In late 1982 British Midland was awarded a licence to offer a London service using DC-9s in competition with the British Airways shuttle, which brought benefits to the travelling public. More expansion was begun in 1987 to provide a greater apron space and other improvements, but at the end of the decade work began on a major extension to the terminal building in order to accommodate the influx of transatlantic flights. By 1990 a new forecourt road system was in use while a new short-term car park had been opened. When the £55 million project is completed in 1992 there will be 70% more space for passengers which are forecast to total 5.5 million by the mid-1990s.

In the meantime the terminal is frequently severely congested due to the somewhat premature transfer of the long haul services and ITs from Prestwick. While Glasgow is ideally located for European and domestic flights, it is a pity that its long-established near-neighbour was not allowed to continue in its familiar role.

Location and access: Situated 10 miles west of Glasgow alongside the M8 at Junction 28. Car park charges graduated. There is a short stay park to the right of the terminal, the charges escalating rapidly after the basic period. An express coach service from the airport to the city centre (Central and Queen Street stations) operates every 30min taking about 20min for the journey. It then continues to Edinbugh where it arrives 1½hr later. By rail from Glasgow Central to Paisley (Gilmour Street) takes 11min. A local bus runs every 10min to the airport from Paisley and less frequently from Renfrew

Terminal: All types of catering are available ranging from quick snacks to full meals. One buffet is open 24hr. There are two bars in the public section of the terminal plus another open 24hr in the international departure lounge. A number of shops offering a wide selection of goods have been provided during the various building extensions

Spectator facilities: None provided. Viewing not encouraged from within the terminal and in any case it is virtually impossible. With the skyline constantly changing as builders' huts appear, external vantage points also regularly vary in usefulness. Better views and photographs can be obtained through the perimeter fence near to the runway thresholds. It is to be hoped that an area will be provided when the terminal is completed, not only for those wishing to indulge in waving at departing relatives, but also for interested visitors. Such a facility had been available for years at Prestwick and is sorely missed

Operators: Scheduled services by Aer Lingus (Boeing 737, Fokker 50), Air Canada (TriStar, Boeing 767), Air France (Boeing 737), Air UK (BAe 146), American Airlines (Boeing 767), British Airways (Boeing 757, BAe 748/ATP, One-Eleven, TriStar), British Midland (DC-9, BAe ATP, Boeing 737), Brymon Airways (Dash Eight), Icelandair (Boeing 737), JAT (Boeing 727), Loganair (Short SD3-60, Twin Otter, BAe 146/ATP), Lufthansa/RFG (ATR-42), Manx Airlines (Short SD3-60, BAe ATP), Northwest Airlines (DC-10), SAS (DC-9)

Charter and IT operators: Adria Airways (MD-80), Aeroflot (Tu-134), Air Atlantis (Boeing 737), Air Europa (Boeing 737), Air Malta (Boeing 737, Airbus A320), Airtours (MD-83), Air Transat (TriStar), Air UK Leisure (Boeing 737), Air 2000 (Boeing 757), American Trans Air (TriStar, Boeing 757), Aviogenex (Boeing 727/737), Balair

(MD-80), Balkan (Tu-134/154), Birmingham European (One-Eleven), Britannia (Boeing 737/767), British Airways (Boeing 757), British Midland (DC-9, Boeing 737), Canadian 3000 (Boeing 757), Dan-Air (One-Eleven), Icelandair (DC-8, Boeing 727/737), JAT (Boeing 727/737), Lineas Aéreas Canarias (MD-80), Monarch Airlines (Boeing 737/757), Oasis (MD-80), Spanair (MD-80), Tunis Air (Boeing 737)

Movements (1989): Total 107,871 (air transport 66,761/club 21,775/private 6,191/empty positioning 7,559). Total passengers 3,959,880
Runways: 05/23 (8,720ft/2,658m) 10/28 (3,570ft/1,088m)
Radio frequencies: 118.8MHz (Tower)/ 119.1MHz (Approach)
Telephone: Glasgow (041) 887 1111
Operated by: Glasgow Airport Ltd

Gloucestershire (Staverton)

The present airport at Staverton was opened in the summer of 1936, allowing the introduction of scheduled services by Railway Air Services on routes to Birmingham, Bristol, Southampton and Weston-super-Mare. The Air Ministry also took an interest, resulting in the erection of additional buildings to accommodate recruits passing through.

During the war Staverton was the home of several training schools, both advanced and elementary. It also housed the Rotol Flight Test Unit plus Folland and Flight Refuelling, both very active companies engaged in development work for the Air Ministry.

Peace brought a rapid reduction in Service activity, until the airfield was finally left

to civilian interests. Murray Chown Aviation took over control in 1949, services to Jersey and Newquay commencing in 1951. At the end of the next year, the whole operation passed to Cambrian Airways. The Welsh carrier continued the Jersey service, although routed it via Southampton for Customs purposes. It had the added benefit of providing a connection with the airline's Paris flight. By 1957 however Cambrian had withdrawn, management of the airfield becoming the responsibility of Smiths Industries, a company associated with Staverton for many years.

Cambrian's successor was Derby Airways who carried on the now traditional Channel Islands operation. The airline's name change to British Midland did not affect the service, continuing until the end of the 1970 season. At this point Intra Airways took over ensuring that the airport's association with the Dakota and the Channel

Islands continued until 1979 when after a route swap, Dan-Air became the licence holder, employing BAe 748s. In addition the airline introduced a seasonal link with the Isle of Man with the same type of aircraft. This arrangement did not last long, with the Guernsey and Jersey routes passing to Guernsey Airlines in 1981, the Isle of Man being dropped from the schedules. The surviving services were also reduced to weekends only during 1982, a frequency subsequently maintained each summer until 1987. Thereafter the sorties were regarded as IT charter flights with the responsibility passing to Brymon and Capital. In 1990 the contract to carry the tour operator's clients to the Channel Islands was won by Celtic Air which proposed to use SD3-30s for the purpose. Problems with licensing meant that the task reverted to Capital, but following this carrier's demise at the end of June yet another change was necessary. This time Aurigny took over the movements with its SD3-60, an arrangement which continued until the end of the relatively short season.

Staverton became the site for Skyfame, the first purely aviation museum set up by Mr Peter Thomas in 1963. However, in 1978 the Collection was forced to leave the airfield, fortunately many of the possessions finding a new home at Duxford.

Location and access: Situated off the B4063 Gloucester to Cheltenham road, the airport entrance being in Bamfurlong Lane. It is about halfway between the two towns. The A40 and M5 Junction 11 are adjacent although there is no direct link to the airport

Terminal: Contains small waiting area. Bar and refreshments available in nearby building

Spectator facilities: A grassed area equipped with seats alongside the entrance road gives a good viewing position. Good landing shots can be obtained when runway 27 is in use from the same vantage point. In both cases a telephoto lens is necessary for most types likely to be seen, although a standard lens will suffice for airliners landing on 27

Operators: Regular IT charter services to Channel Islands on a seasonal basis. Residents include aircraft of Cotswold Aero Club and those of private owners. Staverton also attracts a steady number of light aircraft movements

Movements (1989): Total 87,671 (air transport 578/club 67,006/private 11,382). Total passengers 5,621

Runways: 09/27 (4,662ft/1,421m), 04/22 (3,189ft/972m)

Radio frequencies: 125.65MHz (Tower and Approach)/122.9MHz (Radar)

Telephone: Churchdown (0452) 712005

Operated by: Gloucester and Cheltenham Joint Airport Committee

Guernsey

The island was much slower than neighbouring Jersey to accept civil aviation, since it was 1939 before the airport was opened at La Villiaze. After the German occupation, Channel Islands Airways resumed its operations, only to have them taken over by BEA in 1947. Despite some improvements during the military control period, the grass field was still often waterlogged. No attempt was made to eliminate the problem until it became an economic necessity for BEA to withdraw its last Dakotas from service. In 1961 the Guernsey authorities reluctantly agreed to construct a runway, therefore permitting the regular use of Viscounts.

Although NLM has employed a Fellowship on its seasonal Amsterdam service for the past 13 years without undue comment from the local population, due to runway length and noise restrictions turboprops have always been favoured. However, a new era began in December 1987 when Air

UK supplemented its Friendships with a BAe 146, a type which has since proved very popular. In a similar manner to Jersey, the airport closes at night, until the newspaper flights signal the start of a new day. By no means as busy as its more commercialised neighbour, Guernsey is served by many of the UK airlines direct, but in any case travel via Jersey is simple using Aurigny's frequent inter island links.

The 1980 shuffle of routes following the British Airways decision to relinquish those unprofitable, left Guernsey in the hands of Air UK as the main operator to the UK. Both London airports became the preserve of Heralds, while the Southampton sector saw both Heralds and Friendships on the route. However, late in 1982 it was announced that the Guernsey-Gatwick route licence was to be transferred to Guernsey Airlines from the following April. A certain amount of political pressure was suspected although the reasons given were that the equipment used was shabby. There were no comments made about the stability of the replacement SD3-30s compared with the Herald and Friendship after the changeover. With the sale of the airline to British Air Ferries, Viscounts and Heralds became readily available to take over when necessary, the route prospering under the new management. In conjunction with its parent company, Guernsey Airlines steadily gained more licences to serve a large number of regional airports in the UK, linking them mainly on a seasonal basis to Guernsey and Jersey. In 1987 a Short SD3-60 joined the smaller 330s, all three supporting the Viscount on the busy summer routes. Despite the success of the business, there was a slack period during the winter months which caused a cash flow problem. In an effort to acquire more capital, Guernsey Airlines was sold to Aurigny Air Services with effect from 1 October. Initially it was not expected that there would be any obvious changes, the routes and equipment remaining unaltered.

However it was not long before it was announced that the busy Southampton sector was to be dropped by the new owners. Naturally it produced a number of requests for the licence, with Air Atlantique eventually taking over in May 1988. One season with schedules proved sufficient for the company, so in the spring of the following year it was Jersey European that added the Southampton-Guernsey link to its growing network. Meanwhile Air UK had improved its image and in late 1986 introduced a Friendship 500 on the Heathrow sector, thereby offering another six seats on each flight. One year later the service was further upgraded by the arrival of the BAe 146, this type also taking over some of the Southampton work in due course. Unfortunately rising costs forced the airline to revert to the Friendship in order to maintain frequencies. Jets therefore remain relatively uncommon at Guernsey.

In the autumn of 1989 Guernsey Airlines was merged into Air Europe Express leaving Aurigny to concentrate upon its well established inter-island activities. The company added a Short SD3-60 to its fleet in May 1990 following the need for greater capacity on some routes, the repainting and overhaul work on the ex-Maersk specimen being carried out at Guernsey by Anglo-Normandy Aeroengineering.

Regular freight flights are operated by Channel Express carrying locally grown produce to the mainland in its Heralds and Electras, while a considerable amount of traffic is generated by company, private and club aircraft.

Location and access: Situated 3 miles southwest of St Peter Port off Forest Road. Car park charges graduated. Regular bus services connect the airport with St Peter Port bus station taking about 25min for the journey

Terminal: Contains buffet, bar, lounge and shop

Spectator facilities: External stairs to the terminal roof which provides a very good vantage point for viewing and photography. Admission free. Other vantage points exist around the perimeter of the airport

Operators: Scheduled services by Air France/Brymon (Dash Seven), Air UK (Friendship), Aurigny Air Services (Islander, Trislander, Short SD3-60), British Midland (BAe ATP), Brymon Airways (Dash Seven, Dash Eight), Crossair (Saab SF340), Jersey European (Friendship), KLM CityHopper (Fokker 50, Fellowship), Loganair (BAe ATP, BAe 146), Lufthansa/DLT (Fokker 50)

Charter and freight operators: British Air Ferries (Viscount, Herald), Channel Express (Herald, Electra)

Movements: (1989): Total 67,976 (air transport 48,161/club 11,273/private 4,719). Total passengers 925,868
Runway: 09/27 (4,800ft/1,463m)
Radio frequencies: 119.95MHz (Tower)/ 128.65MHz (Approach)/ 118.9MHz (Radar)
Telephone: Guernsey (0481) 37766
Owned by: States of Guernsey

Heathrow

The site was earmarked for an airfield in 1928 by Fairey Aviation. It became operational two years later with the name of the Great West Aerodrome. Although taken over by the RAF during the war, it was not until May 1944 that work started on the reconstruction programme. The problems of securing funds in wartime for a civil venture dictated the design. It was supposedly intended for the use of Transport Command which meant that the designers were forced to adopt the familiar triangular pattern for the runways. It was so arranged that the airport could be expanded in stages, each causing as little interference as possible during construction.

Transport Command did take over for a short time in October 1945 when a number of officers and men arrived to ready the station for service. On 6 December the Lancastrian G-AGWG of British South American

Airways landed prior to a proving flight to South America. This aircraft also made the first official flight from Heathrow on 1 January 1946 using the one completed runway.

Development continued from that point allowing the opening of the centre terminal area in the mid-1950s, accessible via twin tunnels from the north side. The new complex gradually replaced the inferior temporary accommodation which had been used by long haul passengers for many years.

Heathrow has become one of the world's leading international airports with over 70 airlines providing routes to all parts of the globe. The majority of the movements are those of scheduled services which carry over 23 million passengers annually. Executive aircraft are regular visitors, while the cargo facility opened in 1968 handles the considerable freight traffic generated by British Airways and many foreign airlines. As early as 1973 statistics were already giving a warning that passenger figures were steadily increasing each year, even allowing for the occasional hiccup due to the fuel crisis and recession. Overall the picture was one of growth with saturation point becoming closer. A new terminal was urgently required, but there was no more space in the centre island. Breaking away from this layout was the only solution leading to the start of Terminal 4 in September 1981. Opened to traffic in April 1986, it now handles all BA's intercontinental services together with the airline's Paris,Amsterdam and Athens schedules. Also accommodated in the new premises are KLM, NLM and Air Malta.

Location and access: Situated 14 miles west of central London with access direct from the M4 at Junction 4 or the A4 to the central area. Terminal 4 is alongside the A30 and can be reached from the M25. Each of the four terminals has its own short-term car park with graduated charges. Long-term parking is available on the northern boundary for those using Terminals 1, 2 and 3 while Terminal 4 has its own nearby. A dedicated park for spectators is also situated on the northern perimeter with a frequent bus shuttling backwards and forwards to the Queen's Building. This should be used in view of the cost and congestion in the centre. Bearing in mind the amount of public transport available, it is cheaper to leave a car outside and travel by bus or train. The Piccadilly Line trains from London travel in a clockwise direction around the loop formed by Hatton Cross, Terminal 4 and the centre area before returning to the capital via Hatton Cross. Journey time from London averages about 47min. Numerous local buses call at the airport central bus station to serve all four buildings. Coaches to most parts of the country either leave Heathrow or via a direct link with Victoria coach station. Express services are operated on this route by Fleetline 767 and London Transport's Airbus which also visits Euston railway station. London Country has a direct Speedlink coach linking Gatwick and Heathrow every 20min, while Jetlink 747 has a similar purpose but also includes Luton in its itinerary. For full information telephone 081-668 7261

Terminals: All four have lounge areas, shops, restaurant, bars, buffets, bank and post offices. Terminal 4 has fewer facilities in the public area. Terminal 1 handles all British Airways (European Division) plus all other UK airlines together with Aer Lingus, Cyprus Airways, El Al, Icelandair, Sabena and South African Airways. Following the opening of Terminal 4 several other carriers were relocated

Spectator facilities: A large roof garden is provided over Queen's Building and Terminal 2. It has its own buffet, bar and shops and is open daily from 10am until dusk. There is an admission charge. It is a fine vantage point for viewing, all movements being visible although some are very distant, making binoculars essential. Unfortunately through the years the photographic opportunities have declined, mainly due to the growth of buildings along the front of the terminal. Nowadays shots are limited to a small number of stands, any others requiring the services of a telephoto lens for aircraft on taxiways. However, this is satisfactory for those who did not experience the better times, but sunny conditions can produce difficulties due to glare and heat haze

Operators: Scheduled services by Aer Lingus (Boeing 737), Aeroflot (IL-62/86, Tu-154), Aerolineas Argentinas (Boeing 747), Air Algerie (Boeing 727/737), Air Canada (Boeing 747/767, TriStar), Air France (Airbus A300/A310, Boeing 727/737, ATR-42, Fellowship), Air India (Boeing 747), Air Malta (Boeing 737, Airbus A320), Air Mauritius (Boeing 747SP/767), Air UK (Friendship, BAe 146), Air Zaire (DC-10), Alitalia (MD-80, DC-9, Airbus A300), American Airlines (DC-10, Boeing 767), Austrian Airlines (MD-80, Balkan (Tu-154), Bangladesh Biman (DC-10), British Airways (Boeing 737/747/757/767, Concorde, One-Eleven, TriStar, Airbus A320), British Midland (DC-9, BAe ATP, Boeing 737), British West Indian Airways (TriStar), Brymon Airways (Dash Seven, Dash Eight), CSA-Czechoslovakian Airlines (IL-62, Tu-134), Cyprus Airways (Airbus A310/320), Dan-Air (One-Eleven), Delta Air Transport (BAe 146, Fellowship), Egyptair (Airbus A300), El Al (Boeing 747/757/767), Ethiopean Airlines (Boeing 767), Finnair (MD-80, DC-9, Boeing 737), Ghana Airways (DC-10), Gulf Air (TriStar, Boeing 767), Iberia (Boeing 727, DC-9/10, MD-80, Airbus A300/320), Icelandair (Boeing 737), Iranair (Boeing 747SP), Iraqi Airlines (Boeing 747), Japan Airlines (Boeing 747), JAT (DC-9, Boeing 727/737), Kenya Airways (Airbus A310), KLM (Boeing 737, Airbus A310, DC-10), KLM CityHopper (Fokker 50,

Fellowship), Kuwait Airways (Boeing 747/767, Airbus A310), LOT-Polish Airlines (Tu-134, Tu-154, IL-62), Lufthansa (Airbus A300/310/320, Boeing 727/737), Luxair (Boeing 737, Fokker 50), Malaysian Airlines (Boeing 747, DC-10), Malev (Tu-134/154), Middle East Airlines (Boeing 707), Manx Airlines (BAe ATP/146), Nigeria Airways (DC-10, Boeing 747), Olympic Airlines (Boeing 727, Airbus A300), Pakistan International (Boeing 747), Pan Am (Boeing 727/747, Airbus A310), Qantas (Boeing 747), Royal Air Maroc (Boeing 727/737), Royal Jordanian Airlines (TriStar, Boeing 747), Sabena (Boeing 737, Fellowship), SAS (DC-9, MD-80), Singapore Airlines (Boeing 747), South African Airways (Boeing 747), Sudan Airways (Tristar, MD-80), Saudi Arabian Airlines (Boeing 747), Swissair (MD-80, Airbus A310, Fokker 100), TAP-Air Portugal (Boeing 727/737, TriStar,

Airbus A310), Tarom (One-Eleven, Tu-154), Thai International (Boeing 747), Trans Mediterranean (Boeing 707), TWA (Boeing 747/767, TriStar), Tunisair (Boeing 727/737), THY-Turkish Airlines (Boeing 727, Airbus A310), United Airlines (Boeing 747/767), Varig (DC-10), Viasa (DC-10), Virgin Atlantic (Boeing 747), Zambia Airways (DC-10)

Movements (1989): Total 368,391 (air transport 347,983, private 11,984, empty positioning 8,305). Total passengers 39,881,922

Runways: 09R/27L (12,000ft/3,658m), 09L/27R (12,802ft/3,902m), 05/23 (7,733ft/2,357m)

Radio frequencies: 118.7MHz, 118.5MHz (Tower)/119.2MHz, 119.5MHz, 120.4MHz (Approach)

Telephone: (081) 759 4321

Operated by: Heathrow Airport Ltd

Humberside (Kirmington)

Construction work at Kirmington started in 1941, reaching a point when it was possible for a handover to Bomber Command in October 1942. During the first few months Wellingtons of No 150 Squadron were in residence, joined at the year's end by similar aircraft from No 140 Squadron. Sections

of both merged in late January 1943 to form No 166 Squadron, this unit thereafter taking part in many of the war's major raids. In September that year, Lancasters were received, the type flown for the remainder of the squadron's existence. Over 27,000 tons of bombs were dropped by the unit, plus the laying of 333 tons of mines. After the last operational mission on 25 April 1944 when

24 of its aircraft attacked Berchtesgaden, the squadron was employed on supply runs and POW return ferry flights until disbanding in November 1945.

With its residents gone, Kirmington was quickly run down. After a spell on care and maintenance from February 1946, the site was allowed to be reclaimed as farmland. In the mid-1960s the Lindsey District Council considered the dilapidated airfield for possible redevelopment as the regional airport. Much reconstruction was necessary, but light aircraft began using the site again although even in 1968 there were only 236 movements. Gradually these increased, air taxi companies such as Humber Airways helping things along.

It was March 1974 before the passenger terminal was completed and another year before Humberside Airport, as Kirmington was now known, was served by a scheduled flight. Air Anglia had earlier frequently used the airport for its air taxi work, so it was not surprising that the airline created an outstation at Kirmington. The first route opened was to Amsterdam on 7 April 1975, followed later in the month by a weekend service to Jersey. Subsequently Air Anglia introduced links with Birmingham, Glasgow, Heathrow, Norwich and Teesside. With minor variations such services continued to the time of the formation of Air UK.

The steady expansion began to slow soon after the newly created airline took over the operations. The Birmingham and Teesside routes were dropped, while those to Glasgow and Heathrow were taken over by Eastern Airways initially employing DC-3s. However, it was not long before new equipment was introduced in the form of the Short SD3-30. The airline's main base was established at Humberside using the engineering facilities originally utilised by Air Anglia's outstationed Navajos.

In October 1982 the airline merged with Genair and Casair, although the combined fleet of SD3-30s and Bandeirantes became the responsibility of the Humberside headquarters. The benefits soon became evident with several new routes introduced in addition to expanding the Gatwick service into a direct operation on some timings. For a short time, therefore, Genair was Britain's leading commuter airline, but sadly it was a position that was relinquished in June 1984 when trading was ceased. As usual licences were reallocated, some going to Air Ecosse with Air UK taking back the Humberside-Heathrow sector.

Meanwhile, this carrier continued to ply its Aberdeen, Amsterdam and Edinburgh routes which were the only others on offer at the time. After a brief period at Humberside, Air Ecosse left its services in the hands of Casair, until this company was forced to terminate its operations in March 1988. The airport's Danish link was re-established by Cimber Air in 1987, initially using an ATR-42 for the regular runs until the smaller Nord 262 was found to be adequate for the fairly thin route to Esbjerg. In 1990 the airline decided to drop the schedule which was formally transferred to Newair, a Jetstream operator based at Copenhagen. In the meantime Humberside became the headquarters of Skyrover, which began a schedule in 1989 between the airport and Düsseldorf with the help of a leased Bandeirante. At the outset loads were very encouraging and soon prompted a change to the larger SD3-30. Unfortunately, as winter approached, so traffic rapidly declined to bring the inevitable suspension. It was intended to launch a new service to Esbjerg in the spring of 1990, but the licence was not forthcoming and in any case the route would not support two carriers.

Although such transport types as the Caravelle, Boeing 737, Viscount and Fellowship have been seen at Humberside through the years, the airport has not featured prominently in tour operators' programmes. In 1987 the terminal was extended to provide more accommodation for passengers and to separate the commercial traffic from the busy oil-related helicopter movements. Further airport expansion was due to commence in 1991 with the main attention focused on the runway. By increasing the length by 500m to 2,200m and enhancing the lighting and navigation aids, it is hoped that a greater number of charter flights will use the facilities when completed in 1992. At present potential IT travellers are forced to use Leeds, East Midlands or Manchester, so an increase in choice at Humberside would undoubtedly be welcome.

Location and access: Situated 15 miles east of Scunthorpe alongside A18. The M180 motorway Junction 5 is 3 miles from the airport connecting with the direct link to the Humber bridge. Via this route Hull is about 20 miles distant. Car park has graduated charges. Lincolnshire Road Car Co bus runs from Scunthorpe and Grimsby

taking 45min approximately from each at two hourly intervals
Terminal: The single-storey building contains buffet, bar, shop and lounge area
Spectator facilities: None provided. Viewing is possible through the security fence bordering the northern side of the apron. Photographs can be obtained from this vantage point although afternoons present better opportunities on sunny days. As an alternative the large windows overlooking the apron can be used since the glass is decidedly cleaner than at some locations elsewhere. Landing shots are possible of aircraft using runway 21
Operators: Scheduled services by Air UK (Short SD3-60, Friendship), Newair (Jetstream)

Charter and IT operators: Brymon Airways (Dash Seven)
Bond Helicopters are based at Humberside for the purpose of servicing the numerous oil and gas rigs in the North Sea. The company's Dauphins provide regular movements throughout the day
Movements (1989): Total 47,740 (air transport 13,690/club 16,396/private 7,289). Total passengers 153,235
Runways: 03/21 (5,098ft/1,574m – to be extended by 1,640ft/500m), 09/27 (3,458ft/1,054m)
Radio frequencies: 118,55MHz (Tower)/123.15MHz (Approach)
Telephone: Barnetby (0652) 688456
Operated by: Humberside International Airport Ltd

Inverness (Dalcross)

Civil flying was carried out prewar from a small field beside the Moray Firth about one mile north of Inverness. The present airport at Dalcross was built for the RAF at the beginning of the war, for most of its early life serving as a base for an advanced flying training and gunnery school. It passed to Fighter Command towards the end of the war, becoming a civil airfield in 1947. Nevertheless it reverted to military training again in the early 1950s when the Oxfords of 8 FTS arrived as a result of the demand for pilots in the expanding RAF.

Scheduled services have been continued through the years by BEA, British Airways and more recently Loganair, movements having increased considerably thanks to the oil business requirements. Runway improvements during 1974 enabled British Airways to include One-Elevens and Tridents on some of the London timings. The route was relinquished by the airline in 1983, the successor being Dan-Air. A terminal extension was carried out in 1979 to deal with the upsurge in traffic, at the same time the opportunity was taken to run a campaign to encourage greater use of the airport by airlines and tour operators alike.

Air taxi and charter operations are carried out by Aberdeen Airways, while in addition to the locally based clubs, training aircraft from Perth and privately owned machines also use the facilities. Visits are also made by larger transports such as foreign registered Friendships from time to time. Military aircraft are not an uncommon sight.

Location and access: Situated 8 miles northeast of Inverness off A96 from which it is signposted. Car park charges graduated. Coaches to Inverness connect with flights

Terminal: Single storey building containing bar, buffet and small lounge area

Spectator facilities: None provided. Good views can be obtained from within the terminal, although photography is impeded by the tinted glass. It is possible to find other vantage points for this purpose

Operators: Scheduled services by British Airways (BAe 748), Loganair (Twin Otter, Short SD3-60), Dan-Air (One-Eleven). Non scheduled movements by Bristow Helicopters (S-61, Puma, Bell 212), Aberdeen Airways (Titan, Super King Air), Business Air (Bandeirante)

Movements (1989): Total 21,899 (air transport 6,459/club 10,609/training 927/military 1,636). Total passengers 210,750

Runways: 06/24 (6,191ft/1,887m) 12/30 (2,296ft/700m). Taxiways not in use apart from those from the apron to runways 06 and 12

Radio frequency: 122.6MHz (Tower and Approach)

Telephone: Inverness (0463) 232471

Operated by: Highland and Island Airports Ltd

Ipswich

Created at a time when airfield provision was becoming fashionable, Ipswich was officially opened by the Prince of Wales on 26 June 1930. Used initially by the Suffolk Aero Club, the site was taken over by the Whitney Straight Corporation in 1936. Its aircraft were used for exercises with both the Army and Observer Corps until the war, joined in 1938 by a detachment of the Civil Air Guard. As a satellite for nearby Wattisham, Ipswich

quickly received some of the station's Blenheim IVs as the squadrons dispersed in September 1939. Generally they returned home when needed for operations, but a few sorties were flown from their temporary home in February/March 1941. A change of owner took place in the spring of 1942 when Martlesham Heath took control, leading to a succession of short visits by Spitfire units.

Promotion came in March 1943 when Ipswich was elevated to full RAF Station status, but its involvement with operations ended. Instead it became the base for a motley collection of target-towing flights equipped with Henleys and Martinets. For much of the time the machines ambled along the Essex and Suffolk coast inviting the naval gunners around the Harwich area to demonstrate their skills, a pursuit which continued until 1945. At various times the Army installed some of its Auster IIIs on the airfield, but these departed at the time of D-Day in 1944. Ipswich had little to offer the peacetime RAF, so the Air Ministry quickly put it on a Care and Maintenance basis in August 1945, before releasing the site for civil flying during the following year.

Club and private flying was resumed, there being little to attract the attentions of commercial operators at that stage. At Southend, East Anglian Flying Services (EAFS) was steadily expanding its charter activities during the late 1940s, supplementing this business with a few seasonal schedules to Ostend and Jersey. In 1953 the company received authority to launch an Ipswich-Southend-Rochester-Shoreham-Jersey service, while an Ipswich-Southend-Calais route was approved later that year. East Anglian decided to lease Ipswich Airport from the Corporation from 1 April 1954, the number of destinations on offer increasing considerably as a result of the connections available at Southend. Rapides had been used exclusively until the mid-1950s, but the need for more capacity then brought some Doves into the fleet. Both types became regular sights at Ipswich where the airline also established the East Anglian Flying Club equipped with Austers and Tiger Moths.

By the 1960s larger types were in service, DC-3s operating some of the flights from the airport. They carried the livery of Channel Airways, the name officially adopted by EAFS on 29 October 1962, although the title had been used by the company for many years. Modernisation programmes in the mid-1960s saw the arrival of HS748s to replace the DC-3s, the new type taking over the schedules from Ipswich. However, it was not for long. Two landing accidents at Portsmouth on 15 August 1967 hastened the end of the type's scheduled operations from grass-covered airports, although Herons and Doves continued to visit the Suffolk field to provide feeder links with Southend. Equipped with Viscounts, One-Elevens, Tridents and Comets at the end of the decade, Channel had little interest in Ipswich with its limited potential. Therefore

when the carrier ceased trading in February 1972 it had little effect on the airport. Herons were still to be seen but in the colours of Peters Aviation based at Norwich. No one it seemed was willing to offer schedules, presumably on the assumption that travellers were prepared to make use of the facilities available at Norwich and Stansted, both some distance from Ipswich.

For the next 14 years or so the airport was deprived of regular flights, the terminal building settling down to quietly deteriorate. In the meantime industrial development in the area had greatly increased the demand for air links, so it was with this in mind that Suckling Airways was formed. Originally licences were sought to serve both Amsterdam and Rotterdam on a triangular course using a Twin Otter, but with the application modified to include Manchester, this type became unsuitable. Instead a Dornier 228 was acquired to ply the routes awarded by the CAA, the inaugural sortie to Schiphol taking place on 15 May 1986. Although Rotterdam was not included in the initial programme, it was intended to add this important centre to the company's network as soon as feasible. Such a service certainly seems likely to succeed in view of the void left by the demise of Holland Aero Lines early in 1987. However, Suckling decided against the expansion to concentrate its resources on its existing routes. Normally Ipswich has an excellent, well drained grass surface and at the time was one of few to accommodate scheduled services without the benefit of a hard runway. Unfortunately the persistent downpours during the winter of 1987/88 tested its ability to accommodate the regular movements of the Dornier which steadily introduced a network of ruts and indentations. The situation quickly deteriorated until it became necessary to close the airport. Suckling managed to transfer its terminal to RAF Wattisham as a temporary expedient, but intended to return to Ipswich as soon as possible.

This proved more difficult than expected because the airfield's operator refused permission in view of the damage likely to be caused by the 228's narrow-track undercarriage. In the long term a hard runway was the only solution, but the prospects for this were not good. A new operating base was therefore necessary for Suckling, so after evaluating the various options the airline began flying from Cambridge on 18 July 1988.

Ipswich was therefore deprived of its popular scheduled services with little likelihood of ever enjoying the convenience again. Indeed the very existence of the field was placed in danger of extinction by 1994 following a decision by its Council owners to redevelop the entire site. Various other locations have been suggested for a new airfield to the north of the town, while the conversion of RAF Wattisham is not ruled out if the base ends its military career as a result of defence cuts. One thing is certain: Ipswich needs an airport.

Location and access: Situated 2 miles southeast of Ipswich to the north of the A45(T). A bus links the town centre with the airport entrance every 20min, while a circular route visits hourly
Terminal: Bar and coffee lounge. Refreshments available
Spectator facilities: A grass enclosure is provided in front of the terminal affording excellent views of all movements
Operators: Scheduled services suspended
Movements (1989): Not available
Runways: 08/26 (3,690ft/1,125m grass) 14/32 (3,379ft/1,030m grass)
Radio frequency: 118.325MHz (Tower/Approach)
Telephone: Ipswich (0473) 720111
Operated by: Ipswich Borough Council

Isle of Man (Ronaldsway)

Services to the Isle of Man started in the mid-1930s, flown by several carriers from the mainland. The commercial link with Liverpool was maintained throughout the war although Ronaldsway was used extensively by the RAF and FAA particularly for training purposes. The airfield was returned to the civil authorities in 1946.

BEA took over the passenger services in the following year, which by this time included Liverpool, Blackpool, Carlisle and Glasgow. The network was further expanded by several independents in 1948 working under the Associate Agreement scheme.

For many years the routes remained generally unchanged although they passed through the hands of many different carriers. British Airways continued to serve the Island on a much reduced scale from only London and Manchester until March 1980 when the carrier discontinued many of its domestic routes. As a result the links with Heathrow, Liverpool and Belfast joined the British Midland network, while Air UK took on the Blackpool, Manchester, Glasgow and Dublin sectors on an all-year round basis, with seasonal flights to Jersey, Edinburgh and Leeds. Dan-Air also acquired a share, providing seasonal services between Ronaldsway and Newcastle, East Midlands, Bristol and Gatwick.

Top:
Suckling Airways has established a good record for reliability with its Dornier 228 G-BMMR since moving its UK base to Cambridge.   *AJW*

Above:
Flying training plays a major role at Coventry where Cessna 152 G-BOFM is one of a number used for such a purpose.   *AJW*

Below:
East Midlands is the base of the J. C. Bamford fleet – perhaps better known for its earth-moving vehicles – which includes the BAe 125-800B G-GJCB.   *AJW*

Top:
Twin Otter G-BEJP is one of several used by Loganair for the thinner routes from Edinburgh. *AJW*

Above:
Friendship 500 G-BMXD gets smartly away from Exeter on its way back to Jersey. *AJW*

Below:
Gone are the days when the Viscount was a familiar sight at Guernsey, but the type still occasionally visits on substitute flights or charters. Normally operating the Gambia Air Shuttle, G-AZNA was pressed into service for some weekend work in 1990. *AJW*

It was announced in mid-1982 that a new carrier, Manx Airlines, was to take over the operation of all the Isle of Man services currently flown by Air UK and British Midland. Since it was a joint venture both airlines transferred aircraft to the newcomer to allow operations to begin on 1 November 1982. With a relatively small but effective fleet, Manx quickly gained the support of the islanders at the expense of the sea ferries. Although the company's main routes are those to Heathrow and Liverpool, there are others maintained throughout the year plus those of a seasonal nature. Almost all of the routes to the island are now flown by Manx, the exceptions being those in the hands of Jersey European. During 1987 there were indications that a new airline was being set up at Ronaldsway to offer some competition to Manx, but it did not materialise.

Location and access: Situated 7 miles southwest of Douglas near Castletown. Car park charges gently graduated. The Isle of Man Passenger Transport Board operates regular services connecting the airport with Castletown, Douglas, Port Erin and Port St Mary

Terminal: Contains buffet, bar, restaurant and waiting area

Spectator facilities: A grass area is available on the south side of the terminal and viewing is also possible from within the building

Operators: Scheduled services by: Manx Airlines (Short SD3-60, BAe 146/ATP/ Jetstream), Jersey European (Friendship). Charter and IT flights are occasionally flown

Movements (1989): Total 50,508 (air transport 17,806/club 19,510/private 6,731/test and training 2,297). Total passengers 533,169

Runways: 04/22 (4,153ft/1,266m) 09/27 (5,750ft/1,753m) 18/36 (2,962ft/903m)

Radio frequencies: 118.9MHz (Tower)/120.85MHz (Approach)

Telephone: Castletown (0624) 823311

Operated by: Isle of Man Government Department of Highways, Ports and Properties

Jersey

The present airport was opened on 10 March 1937, replacing the beach landing area at St Aubin's Bay. Numerous scheduled services were operated to the UK and France by Channel Islands Airways up to the German occupation in June 1940, after which time the Luftwaffe made use of the facilities.

In 1945 the prewar carrier resumed operations, but after two years BEA took over the routes. Soon the growing size and number of aircraft using the airport necessitated the provision of a hard runway in 1951/52. This has since been extended at regular intervals to keep pace with the traffic increases as such types as the Viscount, Vanguard and One-Eleven were introduced. The terminal has also been progressively extended to accommodate the corresponding upsurge in passengers.

The Island has also been served by a variety of independent carriers since 1951, including the locally based Jersey Airlines until its absorption into British United (CI) Airways, later British Island Airways, in 1967. Jersey became the headquarters of Intra Airways (now Jersey European) in 1969, scheduled services slowly building up from 1971. Regular inter-island services have been provided by Aurigny Air Services since 1968, the airline later adding Cherbourg to its network.

In 1980 British Airways closed its outstationed facilities on the Island and with it most of the links with the UK. The relinquished routes were taken over by the independent carriers Air UK, Jersey European, Dan-Air and British Midland. In due course further reshuffling within this group allowed a few more airlines the opportunity to fly to Jersey

Of these British Air Ferries and Guernsey Airlines flew both charters and schedules from 14 or so UK regional airports, mainly during the summer season. Jersey tourist authorities maintain a tight control on the number of flights allowed into the Island because obviously there is a limit to the amount of accommodation available for visitors at any one time. For this reason carriers have to submit applications to the CAA in the preceding autumn for the next year's quota. Airlines new to the route jostle for a share in the business, often resulting in special hearings for the cases. One item that cannot be controlled is the weather. Jersey can suddenly be afflicted by sea fog or low cloud making operations impossible. Enormous backlogs can quickly build up in the peak season necessitating extra flights and rearranged schedules once there is a clearance.

While the amount of freight handled at the airport continues to grow, there are no plans to increase the size of the modest cargo terminal. Newspapers are flown to the island by Channel Express which is also responsible for the transport of the flower crop back to the mainland.

The considerable number of movements at Jersey include many light aircraft. The local flying club operates its own machines, but the airport also attracts the attention of many visitors, particularly at weekends during the summer months. Every year, usually on the first weekend in May, an international rally is held to commemorate the liberation in 1945.

Location and access: Situated 5 miles northwest of St Helier off the A12 Beaumont to St Peters road. The airport is adequately signposted. Car park charges graduated. A JMT bus runs every 20min between the airport and Weighbridge Bus Station near the harbour in St Helier. Journey time is about 25min

Terminal: Contains restaurant, buffet, bar, lounge and shop

Spectator facilities: Two sets of external stairs lead to separate areas of the terminal's roof, both of which offer excellent vantage points for viewing and photography.

On sunny days apron shots become more difficult by mid-afternoon, but are by no means impossible. Admission is free. Other very good locations exist towards the ends of the runway and along the northern perimeter. Light aircraft normally park on the grass adjacent to the airport access road, from where many can be photographed over the fence

Operators: Scheduled services by Aer Lingus (Boeing 737), Air France/Brit Air (ATR-42, Fellowship), Air UK (Friendship, BAe 146), Aurigny (Trislander, Short SD3-60), British Airways (One-Eleven, Boeing 737/757), British Midland (Boeing 737, DC-9, BAe ATP, Dash Seven), Brymon Airways (Dash Seven, Dash Eight), Crossair (Saab 340), Dan-Air (One-Eleven, BAe 146), Inter European (Boeing 737), Jersey European (Friendship), KLM CityHopper (Fokker 50, Fellowship), Loganair (BAe 146/ATP), Lufthansa/DLT (Fokker 50, Dash Eight), Manx Airlines (BAe 146/ATP)

Charter and IT operators: Air UK Leisure (Boeing 737), Air Vendee (Dornier 228), Birmingham European (One-Eleven), British Air Ferries (Viscount, Herald), Braathens (Boeing 737), Britannia (Boeing 737), Brymon Airways (Dash Seven, Dash Eight), Stellair (DC-3).

Regular freight flights are made by Channel Express (Herald, Electra)

Movements (1989): Total 97,560 (air transport 58,432/club 19,721/private 15,298). Total passengers 1,890,242
Runway: 09/27 (5,597ft/1,706m)

Radio frequencies: 119.45MHz (Tower)/120.3MHz, 118.55MHz (Approach)
Telephone: Jersey (0534) 46111
Operated by: States of Jersey

Kent International (Manston)

Flying began from the site in 1915 albeit on a fairly limited scale. During the following year the Royal Naval Air Service expanded the facilities, using the airfield mainly for training purposes. Following the formation of the RAF in April 1918 Manston was earmarked as a permanent base. It brought the provision of new buildings to house the influx of more personnel, although the main activities on the airfield were still predominantly concerned with training in some guise.

Its geographical position helped to determine Manston's role at the start of World War 2, which was that of an advanced fighter station. With all the non-operational units dispersed elsewhere, Fighter Command took control in November 1939 thereafter moving its squadrons in and out of what was to become the front line. Subjected to many intensive Luftwaffe attacks, there were times when the airfield was unusable, but by 1941 Manston was able to take a more aggressive role. Although still a

grass airfield, extensions had lengthened the runways which were frequently used by returning aircraft badly damaged in combat. Eventually it was decided to construct a long and wide runway designed specifically to aid the safe arrival of stricken bombers and fighters. Work started in June 1943, operational flying continuing from a temporary grass strip. Despite the size of the task, the contractor expedited the completion of the work to enable the new runway to come into use in April 1944. It was also one of the few in the UK to be equipped with FIDO to permit landings in the densest of fog, a facility which saved many lives before the end of the war.

Transport Command assumed control of Manston in April 1946, Dakotas becoming the main occupants although both freight and personnel also staged through on their way overseas. In 1950 the station reverted to Fighter Command, but only to act as a caretaker pending the arrival of the USAF in July 1950. Various fighter wings then spent periods at Manston, joined at times by search and rescue aircraft. During the eight years or so that the airfield was occupied by the Americans, several construction projects were completed including a batch of new hard-standings.

Under Care and Maintenance for a short time, Manston became the base for Silver City in April 1959, a move made necessary by the closure of Blackbushe. Using Handley Page Hermes, the company flew regular services between Kent and Le Touquet plus an intensive programme of ITs. This activity continued until the spring of 1962 when the airline became a part of the new Gatwick-based British United Airways. Its place at Manston was filled by Air Ferry equipped with Vikings and a DC-4, operations starting on 30 March 1963. In conjunction with Leroy Tours, the airline began to fly ITs to all parts of Europe. A scheduled licence was acquired for a Manston-Verona link, but this was never launched. Taken over by the Air Holdings group in late 1964, the next year saw the carrier operating vehicle ferry services from Manston to Calais, Le Touquet, Ostend and Rotterdam using Bristol Freighters leased from British United. Two DC-6s arrived at the end of 1965 remaining in service until the airline's close down at the end of October 1968.

Another company closely associated with Manston was Invicta Airways. Formed in November 1964, this airline was also involved in IT flights which were started on 20 March 1965 with a trip to Basle. Such was the carrier's success that three DC-4s and two Vikings joined the three-strong fleet for the company's second season. Invicta was also awarded a scheduled licence to link Manston with Ostend, an enterprise launched in May 1966. Three years later a merger with British Midland ended the airline's passenger activities from Manston, but after a short time a new company emerged to resume work at the base. This time Invicta Air Cargo concentrated on freight movements, a pursuit continued until 1971 when passenger charters were restarted with Vanguards. However, most of this flying was carried out from Luton with only an occasional charter operating from Manston, freight remaining the principal occupation at the airport until the demise of Invicta in 1981.

Throughout the period a military presence had continued, Chipmunks and rescue helicopters becoming the normal residents although its role as a diversion airfield was maintained. Manston is also regularly used by RAF and foreign air forces' aircraft on training details or in transit.

In 1982 the civil operation was acquired by Seaborne Aviation, a company intent on expanding the airport's business generally. While executive and privately-owned aircraft use the facilities, there has been little interest shown by airlines. However, British Air Ferries introduced a seasonal Saturdays flight to Jersey in 1984 using one of its Viscounts, a service not only repeated in the following years, but expanded in 1986 to also offer direct links with Guernsey.

Unfortunately BAF was too involved in its own efforts to survive in 1988, so the series was flown by Dan-Air 748s instead. There was another change for the next season when Brymon became the contracted carrier for the weekly Channel Islands routes, but in 1990 Capital took over the responsibility for the Guernsey operation by routeing its 360 via Lydd both inbound and outbound. This arrangement did not last for very long due to the airline's collapse at the end of June, so thereafter passengers were carried on Brymon's Jersey flight.

Since the early 1970s, IT activities from Manston have not been particularly numerous, but in recent years flights to both Yugoslavia and Majorca have been available, albeit on a modest scale. Both Adria and Aviogenex have been employed for the former with Dan-Air positioning a One-Eleven from and to Gatwick for the weekly visit to Palma.

A regular cargo service was begun by Aeron International in 1986, but with the sale of its CL-44s two years later, the airline terminated the visits. In 1990 another freight run was introduced by Tampa Colombia involving a DC-8 arriving every Saturday from Bogota with flowers and fruit. Plans are well advanced for a new 40,000sq/ft warehouse to replace the elderly accommodation currently in use.

Prior to 1989 the terminal facilities were not very impressive, but this all changed with the official opening of a brand new building in October. A simple, but attractive design was chosen which unusually does not resemble a DIY centre. Its spacious interior is ample to cope with existing traffic, but there is room to expand when the need arises. Probably a more urgent requirement is to increase the area of the apron to assist ground manoeuvring.

Even before this development, the title Kent International had been adopted to improve its chances of attracting a greater number of movements, particularly in view of the rapidly growing congestion at other southeast airports. During the summer of

1990 KIA was one of several named as possible candidates to relieve this situation, a duty it could undertake without massive runway construction. Road access is the main problem, but this could be rectified fairly easily. Whether operators could be encouraged to move so far from London is another question. In the past there has always been resistance to using Stansted which is half the distance, but this time there may be no choice.

Location and access: Situated 4 miles west-northwest of Ramsgate. Entrance is on B2050 via A253. It is now signposted as Kent International. Long and short-term car parks, the latter offering the first 4hr free. An East Kent bus runs irregularly from Ramsgate Harbour taking about 20min for the journey
Terminal: Single storey building contains lounge, buffet and bar
Spectator facilities: None provided. A good view of the apron is possible from the clean buffet windows through which photographs can be taken. Almost the same scene can be observed from the long-term car park adjacent to the terminal, but here the familiar chain link fence provides the handicap. Nevertheless photographs are not too difficult to obtain, especially using a 200mm lens. Located opposite the military entrance is a small collection of RAF aircraft
Operators: Non-scheduled services by Brymon Airways (Dash Seven)
Charter and IT operators: Dan-Air (One-Eleven), Aviogenex (Boeing 737), Adria (DC-9), Air Atlantis (Boeing 737). Scheduled freight services by Tampa Colombia (DC-8). Other cargo flights are handled, particularly those operated by African States. There are also a number of movements generated by 707s undergoing overhaul
Movements (1989): Total 17,610 (air transport 307/private 4,048/club 12,768). Total passengers 17,085
Runways: 11/29 (9.029ft/2,752m) 06/24 (2,598ft/792m grass)
Radio frequencies: 128.775MHz (Tower)/126.35MHz (Approach)
Telephone: Manston (0843) 823333
Owned by: Ministry of Defence. Civil operator Kent International Ltd

Land's End (St Just)

Prior to the mid-1930s travellers to the Scilly Isles were forced to entrust themselves to the ship which regularly linked the Islands with Penzance. Always a lively stretch of water, the four-hour journey was something of an endurance test. There was obviously scope for an air service, but it was 1935 before proving flights were introduced using some land between Sennen and St Just for the mainland terminal. Needless to say the enterprise met with approval, especially since the trip over the water was completed in 20min. As a result, Land's End Airport was opened in September 1937 to handle the scheduled service offered by Channel Air Ferries. Later this carrier became a part of the Great Western & Southern Airlines (GW&S) which not only continued the operation, but increased the frequency using Dragons G-ACPY and G-ADDI. In May 1939 the airline added Plymouth and Bristol to the route, while Western Airways began a new service linking St Just with Newquay, Barnstaple and Swansea.

At the outbreak of war all commercial flying was suspended, but it was not long before it was realised that the Islands needed regular communications in view of their strategic importance, so the Dragons resumed work. One aircraft was delegated for exercises with the Army, leaving the second (G-ACPY) to cope with the return trips to St Mary's, the number varying with the demand. Unfortunately the faithful Dragon was lost en route to St Just on 3 June 1941, believed to be the victim of a Ju88 attack. Once more the service was suspended, to be temporarily reinstated in the autumn. On 4 November, Land's End airfield was closed down completely until May 1945 when the GW&S restarted the schedules, but this time using Rapides.

Postwar policy meant that the carrier became a part of the newly-formed British European Airways, although it was 1 February 1947 before the latter was in a position to take over all the domestic routes and fleets. In the southwest corner of the country the vital link continued, albeit with Rapides in new livery. Despite many attempts to produce a replacement aircraft through the years, there was nothing to surpass the search for operations from airfields such as St Just and St Mary's. Eventually BEA introduced Sikorsky S-61 helicopters on to the route moving the Cornwall terminal to a new heliport on the outskirts of Penzance. Most of the Rapides still in service joined Scillonia, a small airline operating freight and passenger charters from St Just. Schedules were also operated between the airfield, Newquay and the Scillies in the mid-1960s. Re-equipment plans first centred around a pair of Islanders, but these were cancelled before delivery. Instead the airline began negotiations for two Twin Pioneers in Kuwait. In due course the aircraft returned to the UK but their new owner was detained, resulting in the demise of Scillonia. In the 1970s Land's End Aero Club maintained the airfield's links with the Rapide by offering scenic flights in G-AIYR, these coming to an end with the sale of the machine in 1978.

Apart from commercial and club flying, St Just has also been the birthplace of a number of replicas including a full-size Hawker Fury. The first Volmer Sportsman amphibian in the UK was also constructed on the site where many of the buildings date from the early days. In 1986 a new company known as Isles of Scilly Skybus was unsuccessful in winning CAA approval for a scheduled licence to restore the link between St Just and St Mary's. Nevertheless, the airline acquired a pair of Islanders and began freight and passenger charters between the two points. A new application in 1987 was viewed more favourably by the authorities despite objections from British International Helicopters at Penzance. Starting on 6 April an increasing number of return trips were made, until in the three months of July, August and September, six sorties were

flown every day except Sunday. For many travellers the existence of a fixed-wing service as an alternative to the helicopter was welcome and enabled the carrier to increase its frequencies to eight during the subsequent summer seasons. Although loads were satisfactory, they were insufficient to justify the introduction of a larger type such as the Twin Otter, so another two Islanders were acquired from Aurigny during 1989 to take the fleet total to four.

Freight still contributes a considerable amount of business for the company which helps to compensate for the necessary reduction in the number of scheduled flights during the winter months.

Location and access: Situated 6 miles west of Penzance off A30 and south of B3306 from Crows-an-Wra. Ample car parking space charged at a daily rate. Short stays are free. A minibus service to and from Penzance BR station operates hourly for pre-booked passengers. A Cornwall Busways route to Land's End can be used but this involves a 20min or so walk to the airfield from the nearest alighting point

Terminal: A part of the original prewar building, it has been converted to contain a lounge and buffet restaurant with sun terrace facing the airfield

Spectator facilities: None specifically provided, but all movements can be seen from the buffet terrace. A 50mm lens can be used, but a 200mm is necessary for subjects parked on the grass opposite the terrace. There are also suitable vantage points for photography around the perimeter, the location being dependent upon the wind direction

Operators: Scheduled services by Isles of Scilly Skybus (Islander). Various movements by the Land's End-based Aero Club and privately owned aircraft. Westward Airways engineering facility handles maintenance and also the construction of replicas to order

Movements (1990): Figures not reported
Runways: 07/25 (2,221ft/677m), 12/30 (1,699ft/518m), 17/35 (2,598ft/792m) – all grass surface. Public transport flights use 07/25 and 17/35

Radio frequency: 130.7MHz (Tower/Approach)
Telephone: Penzance (0736) 788944
Operated by: Westward Airways (Land's End) Ltd

Leeds/Bradford (Yeadon)

Although opened in October 1931, passenger services did not begin until an extension was completed in 1935. The Envoys of North Eastern Airways then connected the airport with Heston and Newcastle while West Coast Air Services introduced Blackpool and Isle of Man schedules.

Civil flying was suspended at the outbreak of war, September 1939 also seeing the departure of the resident No 609 Auxiliary Squadron to other bases. After becoming an RAF Station, Yeadon passed through the hands of several Groups before Training Command installed the Tiger Moths of 20 EFTS in March 1941. Early the following year this unit was disbanded and the airfield was transferred to the Ministry of Aircraft Production.

The nearby shadow factory was taken over by Avro, who subsequently built thousands of their products including Ansons, Lancasters, Lancastrians, Yorks and Lincolns. It was beneficial to Yeadon since it was necessary to provide runways, taxitracks and hangars to accommodate these aircraft.

After the war ownership passed to the MCA, club flying being restarted by Lancashire Aircraft Corporation, who also reintroduced airline services. The Auxiliary Squadron returned, this time with Mosquitos, but the type gave way to Spitfires before No 609 finally departed in 1950. There was a lull in the activities at

Yeadon after the MCA withdrew, but Yeadon Aviation assumed control after a time and flying recommenced.

Scheduled services were operated by BKS in the mid-fifties, serving Belfast, Düsseldorf, Isle of Wight, Jersey, Ostend and Southend, later adding Edinburgh, Glasgow and London. Another change in the airport administration came in 1959, when the Leeds and Bradford Airport Committee took over full responsibility. Soon afterwards other airlines began to use the airport, Aer Lingus introducing Friendships on a Dublin route, Starways using Viscounts on their Newquay service, while Silver City added Jersey and the Isle of Man to its network. Many of the destinations served by these earlier carriers are covered by the present day operators. In addition to the club, company and private aircraft based at Leeds/Bradford, the movements are increased appreciably by the activities of Northair Aviation, the Cessna agents for the area.

A new runway was added in 1965, while a modern terminal was completed in time for its opening in May 1968. A subsequent extension to runway 15/33 permitted the operation of larger jet aircraft although even this soon proved inadequate. After some ten years of discussions and enquiries, the decision to go ahead with a major expansion programme was taken in January 1981. Work began in 1982 to extend the main runway by 2,000ft/604m and the terminal area to give much improved passenger and freight facilities. When completed it opened the way for transatlantic charters because such types as the 747 and TriStar could then be handled.

Undoubtedly Leeds/Bradford reaped the benefit of having its own locally-based commuter airline. Originally known as Brown Air when operations began in 1983, after adopting the title Capital Airlines in 1987 the company expanded very rapidly until its constantly growing network was maintained by a six-strong fleet of SD3-60s and two BAe 146s. Introducing the latter type was a costly business and sadly it proved more than could be borne by the parent company, so Capital was forced to cease its operations at the end of June 1990. This time the airport was affected adversely both financially and in traffic figures, but it was hoped that a smaller carrier would rise again.

Restricted opening hours have had to be observed by Leeds/Bradford due to objections from the neighbouring residents. Consequently it has meant that some operators have been reluctant to base an aircraft at the airport because of the ban on night movements, although a modest concession in 1989 changed the closing time to 23.00. In the future there is a distinct possibility that Leeds will attract a growing number of business movements, many of which currently use Manchester. This growth will follow the increasing use of the area for conferences and other activities by the business community.

Location and access: Situated 6 miles from both Leeds and Bradford on A658. Car park charges graduated. West Yorkshire routes 50A, 50B, 647 and 747 link the airport with Leeds, Bradford and Otley
Terminal: Contains restaurant, buffet, bar and lounge
Spectator facilities: There is an area on the first floor which overlooks the apron. This gives good views of all movements including those on the main runway. Fronted by tinted glass, photography is therefore less easy but nonetheless not impossible with care. Along the roof edge of a projecting canopy, the presence of a barrier creates an annoying obstruction and appears to serve no useful purpose. There are other vantage points to be found around the perimeter towards the ends of the main runway, while the hill on the south side of the airport also offers opportunities for photography. A 200mm lens is needed for aircraft of Boeing 737 size
Operators: Scheduled services by Aer Lingus (Short SD3-60, Fokker 50), Air UK (Friendship, BAe 146), British Midland (DC-9, Boeing 737), Dan-Air (BAe 146, One-Eleven), Manx Airlines (Short SD3-60 – seasonal), Ryanair (One-Eleven), Loganair (Short SD3-60), Sabena/Delta Air Transport (Brasilia)
Charters and IT operators: Adria Airways (DC-9), Air Europa (Boeing 737), Air Malta (Boeing 737), Air 2000 (Boeing 737/757), Aviogenex (Boeing 737), Balkan (Tu-154), Britannia (Boeing 737), Cyprus Airways (Airbus A310), JAT (Boeing 727), Monarch (Boeing 737), Worldways (TriStar)
Movements (1989): Total 56,757 (air transport 24,631/club 16,870/private 10,311). Total passengers 883,446
Runways: 14/32 (7,400ft/2,250m) 10/28 (3,609ft/1,100m)

Radio frequencies: 120.3MHz (Tower)/ 123.75MHz (Approach)/ 121.05MHz (Radar)

Telephone: Rawdon (0532) 509696
Operated by: Leeds/Bradford Airport Ltd

Liverpool (Speke)

The planning stage began in 1928 with the first experimental passenger service two years later. Apart from a few token flights, transport movements did not increase significantly until 1933 when the airfield was granted an operating licence, although most of the activity was created by the local flying club. From 1934 the number of airlines using Speke gradually increased to include such operators as Railway Air Services, Midland and Scottish, Blackpool and West Coast Air Services, Hillman Airways, United Airways and in 1936 Aer Lingus with a Dublin route. As the traffic increased so the need for better passenger facilities became more urgent. A new terminal was completed in 1939 to cope with the fact that Liverpool had become one of the busiest airports in the UK.

Even before war broke out, Speke had been earmarked for military use, partly as a defence base for Liverpool, but particularly in view of its close proximity to the docks and industry. In 1936 No 611 Squadron moved in with Tutors and Harts, although by the outbreak of war these had been replaced by Battles. A number of fighter squadrons took up temporary residence to protect the city, but the production of Blenheims and Halifaxes by Rootes provided much of the military activity. In addition the factory based at Speke assembled the incoming American built aircraft after their sea crossing of the Atlantic. One distinct benefit derived was the provision of tarmac runways and additional buildings.

Unlike most other airports, Liverpool continued to handle a few civilian flights during the war, namely those to Eire and the Isle of Man operated by Aer Lingus and Railway Air Services.

Postwar domestic routes were taken over by BEA using at various times Avro XIXs, Junkers Ju52s, DC-3s and Rapides, while Aer Lingus continued their Irish service with DC-3s. Liverpool has also produced its own local carriers. For instance Steiner Airways existed with Consuls in the late forties, while Starways later successfully introduced internal scheduled services and ITs employing DC-3s, DC-4s and Viscounts.

Belatedly, control of the airport passed to the Liverpool City Council in January 1961, whereupon development began in earnest.

Runway 09/27 was constructed to meet the modern requirements, backed up by new taxiways and access points. One of the existing runways was extended and further apron area also provided to cater for the expected growth in traffic.

Cambrian Airways took over the Liverpool operations from BEA in the 1960s, continuing until the airline's total absorption into British Airways in 1972, after which the Cambrian name steadily disappeared. Services from Liverpool also declined, until at the end of October 1978 the routes were transferred to British Midland.

With the new operator timings were improved, although gradually the airline was obliged to adjust frequencies, destinations and equipment. Nevertheless there was a greater determination to succeed than had been evident for some years.

In 1979 Liverpool was chosen as the centre of the Post Office mail flight organisation. After a trial period, the operation proved a great success and was soon well established and a building provided for the mail interchange.

The airport once again became the headquarters of an airline when Genair commenced operations in 1981. At first only the Gatwick route was flown, but in 1982 Amsterdam and Newquay were added to the network. Air Ecosse began scheduled services to Scotland, while Jersey European introduced Dublin and Stansted as their contribution although both carriers soon closed down their Liverpool passenger operations. In November 1982 the Isle of Man services were taken over by Manx Airlines formed as a joint effort by Air UK and British Midland, an enterprise which has proved very successful and popular with all apart from the proprietors of the sea ferries.

The closure of the original airfield in mid-1982 concentrated all movements on to the single runway with the resultant lengthy distance to taxy to the terminal. Plans went ahead to provide a new complex; the control tower and apron being the first to be ready for use in the autumn of 1982 and 1983 respectively. Work started on the passenger building in February 1985, taking about one year to complete. Officially opened on 26 March 1986, a further month's work was still necessary before the new facilities could be used by the public. Therefore it was the 07.00 departure of the Manx SD3-60 G-ISLE on 28 April that marked the first movement outbound, the same company's aircraft G-RMSS having the distinction of

becoming the first arrival 90min later.

Thereafter the volume of traffic remained very much the same, the only significant change coming in 1989 when Aer Lingus was forced to end its associations with Liverpool in favour of Ryanair. In the meantime it became known that the airport's owners were interested in selling a major shareholding. After carrying out project studies, British Aerospace duly acquired 76% of the share capital in June 1990, leaving the remainder with the five Merseyside local authorities. A new company was formed called British Aerospace (Liverpool Airport) (BALA) which quickly announced its intention to develop the site as the first major private-sector airport to be constructed in the world. Designed to handle 200,000 movements and over 30 million passengers annually by 2005, the expansion will make use of the undeveloped area surrounding the existing buildings. When necessary a second runway will be built on land reclaimed from the River Mersey. An ambitious project which aims to make Liverpool the northwest gateway to Europe with routes linking the UK with Japan, the US and the near continent.

Location and access: Situated 6 miles southeast of the city off the A561. Car park charges graduated. Trains run every 15min from Liverpool Central to Garston station which is about 1½ miles from the airport. Merseybus services 80 and 89 provide the connection with the airport terminal. From here the former runs at 15min intervals to the city centre while the 89 departs every 30min bound for Garston, Huyton, Prescot and St Helens. National Express service 350 leaves every 2hr for Manchester, Sheffield and Nottingham with certain trips continuing to Cambridge and Clacton
Terminal: Built in a modern style, the building contains a buffet and bar on the first floor overlooking the apron
Spectator facilities: None provided. Nevertheless the large windows in the buffet and waiting area ensure that all movements can be observed. Photographs can be obtained with care through the glass, providing a section can be found that has not been decorated by fingermarks and the like. This hazard almost elevates Liverpool into the same league as Palma and Brussels. Assuming a clear patch has been found, a zoom lens is preferable although the standard variety is sufficient for aircraft parked on near stands. This vantage point is

likely to become crowded at times, making it difficult to secure a convenient spot by a window

Operators: Scheduled services by Manx Airlines (Short SD3-60, BAe ATP/146), British Midland (DC-9), Ryanair (ATR-42, One-Eleven).

Charter and IT operators: Adria Airways (DC-9), Airtours (MD-83), Aviogenex (Boeing 737), Viva Air (Boeing 737), Dan-Air (One-Eleven), TNT (BAe 146 – parcels). Mail flights are made on weeknights by numerous aircraft, with operators changing as contracts expire. Those likely to appear are Woodgate Air Services (Navajo), Gillair (Short SD3-30), Loganair (Twin Otter), Merrix Air (Navajo), Merlin Air Services (Caravan), Channel Express (Herald), BAC

Leasing (Twin Otter), J & J Aviation (Bandeirante), Business Air (Bandeirante, Short SD3-60) and Celtic Air (Short SD3-30).

There are a large number of resident aircraft operated by Liverpool Aero Club, Keenair and Cheshire Flying Training School, plus company and private owners

Movements (1989): Total 87,803 (air transport 20,963/club 46,478/private 2,592/test and training 8,262). Total passengers 476,544

Runway: 09/27 (7,500ft/2,286m)

Radio frequencies: 118.1MHz (Tower)/119.85MHz (Approach)/118.45MHz (Radar)

Telephone: (051) 486 8877

Operated by: Liverpool Airport PLC

London City (STOLport)

For many years the idea of a city-centre airport has appealed to operators but has largely remained a dream. A step nearer was taken in early 1981 when the chairman of the Mowlem construction company discussed the feasibility of such a project with the Chief Executive of the London Docks Development Corporation. It was the centre quay between the Royal Albert and King George V docks that was chosen as the site for such a scheme which would be only one part of the overall redevelopment plans for the derelict area. With the help of Brymon Airways, a trial landing was made by a Dash Seven, even then recognised as the type ideally suited to operations in the space available.

Planning applications were submitted, but in January 1983 it was announced that there would be a public inquiry which was not concluded until October. Even this did not allow much visible progress to be made and it was not until May 1985 that outline planning permission was given. During the waiting period much of the design work continued so the company was in a position to submit the proposals for detailed consent at an early date, approval being received in February 1986. Nevertheless, it was still not possible to start the actual construction because discussions between the Development Corporation and the Port of London Authority lingered on, the obstacle being the ownership of the freehold.

Work eventually started in April, the first task being the demolition of the large warehouses and other buildings standing on the 40-hectare site. Progress was swift so that by Christmas the runway was completed and the terminal shell was roofed over. It was arranged that departing passengers used the first floor holding lounges at the gates before proceeding to the aircraft, seven stands being provided initially with space available for another three in the future. Facilities for those arriving are situated at ground level. As early as 1982, the CAA had to open a pending file as carriers began to lodge their licence applications. Brymon of course was the first in the queue, but was soon joined by such companies as Jersey European, Manx, City Air, British Air Ferries and Brown Air. After more serious thought all of these lost interest, leaving only Brymon and newcomer Eurocity Express as the contenders. Following the hearings the CAA approved both airlines' requests, so when commercial services began on 26 October 1987, it brought a duplication of effort on the Paris sector with Brussels exclusive to Eurocity.

After only a few weeks it became necessary to suspend the schedules to the French capital because of air traffic difficulties, but after a month flights were fully restored. In March 1988 a new name came into use at the airport when Eurocity took the title of London City Airways, at the same time announcing that a link with Amsterdam would be launched in May. There was then a long pause before a third company joined the pioneers at London City, but in September 1989 the Dutch carrier Flexair started operating schedules between the Docklands site and Rotterdam with a Dornier 228. Further international flavour was gained when two of Brymon's Dash Sevens were repainted in full Air France livery for use on new links to Strasbourg and Lille.

The airport's developers had realised from the beginning that in its present state the range of aircraft able to avail themselves of the facilities was strictly limited. It was therefore essential to extend the runway by 169m so that types such as the BAe 146, Fokker 50, ATR-42 and Saab 340 could be handled. Trials with the 146 were carried out in July 1988 and aroused very little adverse comment from the nearby residents, but it was not until 12 September 1989 that the necessary planning applications were submitted. This action motivated the Departments of Transport and the Environment to arrange for a public enquiry to be held during the summer of 1990.

Unfortunately, London City Airways was forced to contract its operation in the spring for economic reasons, with the result that Brymon took over the Amsterdam route.

This move did not solve the situation so on 1 September, British Midland assumed responsibility for London City's remaining activities. At the same time the Paris route was dropped from the network leaving only the Brussels sector, albeit with increased frequency of service.

It was a sad end for the airline which had helped to establish the Docklands site during its first three years of existence. The decision came at a time just as the news was released that objections to the runway extension had been withdrawn. At least it gave fresh hope for the airport's future prospects but was too late for the carrier. In the meantime, newcomer British Independent Airways applied for a scheduled licence to link London City with Pontoise, north of Paris, while Suckling sought approval to operate services to Manchester.

Location and access: Situated 6 miles from the City via A13 and A1011 Silvertown Way at Canning Town roundabout. From the north and east of London use of the M11 and the A406 North Circular gives swift access via a newly completed system of roads to the north of the airport. The routes are well signposted. Both short- and long-term car parks are provided, the latter offering an initial free period but afterwards stays are charged in 24hr periods. British Rail's (Network SouthEast) North London Line serves Silvertown station which is 300m from the airport entrance. Trains give connections with the London Underground at West Ham (District and Metropolitan), Stratford (Central) and Highbury and Islington for the Victoria Line. A dedicated Riverbus operates at 20min intervals on weekdays between Charing Cross Pier, Swan Lane Pier near London Bridge and London City Pier. A shuttle bus then completes the 40min overall journey. Every 20min on Mondays to Saturdays bus route 276 links the airport with the BR stations at West Ham, Canning Town and Stratford. The Docklands Light Railway is a rapid transit system which in stage one links Tower Hill with the southern tip of the Isle of Dogs and Stratford. Future extensions will take the line to a point much nearer to the airport with a connecting bus link provided
Terminal: Contains landside cafeteria and restaurant at the east end of the first floor. Shops and bank on ground floor
Spectator facilities: None provided, but from the cafeteria a view of the runway is possible across the King George V dock.

The ground level car park offers a better vantage point with photography possible using a 200mm lens for the Dash Sevens
Operators: Scheduled services by Brymon Airways/Air France (Dash Seven), British Midland Airways/Sabena (Dash Seven), Flexair (Dornier 228). Occasional pleasure flights and charters by the UK companies at weekends
Movements (1989): Total 11,785 (air transport 10,964/training 291). Total passengers 216,383. Licensed number of movements limited to 120 daily (40 at weekends). It is hoped to increase the weekday total to 130, with the same number at weekends but with a maximum of 90 either Saturday or Sunday
Runway: 10/28 (2,500ft/762m). Ultimate length 3,055ft/931m subject to planning permission
Radio frequencies: 118.075MHz (Tower/128.025MHz (Radar)
Telephone: 071 474 5555
Operated by: London City Airport Ltd

Luton

The grass airfield at Luton was officially opened on 16 July 1938. A need for larger premises had already prompted Edgar Percival to set up his expanding works at the new site in order to increase production of the Vega Gull. This type was developed into the Proctor, which began to appear in late 1939 to serve as RAF communications aircraft. During the war the company produced the type for radio operator training, while the civilianised Mk 5 proved a success amongst the postwar small operators.

Percival's products continued to be adopted by the RAF. The Prentice, Prince variants, Provost and Jet Provost were all designed and in many cases built at Luton.

By the mid-fifties the company was known as Hunting Percival, abbreviated to Hunting before becoming a part of the British Aircraft Corporation. The reorganisation brought aircraft production to an end at Luton.

The Napier engine company was also located on the airfield, while on the lighter side, the Luton Flying Club was re-established as soon as possible after the war. In the 1950s the airfield became the operating base for several charter airlines including Eagle Aviation's three Yorks, which were resident from April 1950 to November 1952. Scheduled services by Derby Aviation were available in 1959, the year that the council planners realised that their airport was beginning to fulfil its intended role. To help speed up the process the decision was taken to construct a new runway 5,423ft in length, a distance in due course extended to 7,078ft. It had the desired effect, encouraging both operators and passengers in such numbers that it soon highlighted the inadequacies of the old wooden terminal building. Consequently a brand new £1 million complex was designed and built ready for its opening in 1966.

One of the newcomers to Luton was Autair, a helicopter operator which had decided to enter the air transport market in 1960 using an ex-BEA DC-3. By the time that the company started work in earnest the following year it had a fleet of three which were kept busy flying ITs. An entry into the scheduled scene was made in 1963 when on 1 October, Viking G-AHPL left the airport on its inaugural trip to Blackpool. Loads proved encouraging, so Autair purchased three Ambassadors to provide increased capacity, all entering service for the 1964 season. To develop its scheduled interests, the carrier acquired BEA's three surplus Heralds, taking over the BKS service from Teesside to London, later extended to Dundee. By 1969 Luton had seen a dramatic increase in the number of IT passengers handled and it was becoming obvious that Autair was clearly more involved in this type of work. As anticipated all schedules were dropped from 31 October and from the beginning of the new year the airline became Court Line. Luton was firmly established as a holiday airport.

As more and more people poured through the terminal so it became more and more inadequate. Then came the wide-bodied TriStars. In 1973 Court took delivery of two, each able to move 400 passengers, which did little to ease the overstretched ground services' problems. During the year a staggering 3,145,658 travellers squeezed through the airport, but it was to be the highest figure for many years. The collapse of Luton's busiest carrier in 1974 reduced the total drastically to 1,920,275 in 1974/75. Although responsible for a major share of the airport's improving fortunes, Court was not alone by any means. Apart from Dan-Air's contribution, both Britannia and Monarch were playing a considerable part in the success story. Nevertheless, the collapse was a serious blow, but it did at least bring some respite and an opportunity for some terminal expansion.

It was to be 1978 before Luton became officially recognised by a Government White Paper as a fully-fledged international airport.

As eventually a capacity of 5 million passengers per annum was envisaged, the Borough Council was sufficiently encouraged to embark on a major development starting in 1979 and taking five years to complete. Finally, when the new facilities were formally opened by the Prince of Wales on 11 July 1985, a far more spacious and modern terminal was ready for service. At this stage the capacity had risen to 3.5 million but the annual total number of passengers passing through was still under 2 million. There was therefore a need to encourage more airlines, especially those with schedules.

These have never been particularly numerous at Luton, for many years only a seasonal British Midland service to Jersey being available. An international route to Brussels was introduced by Euroflite in 1980, followed in February 1985 by a regular link with Amsterdam provided by newcomer London European. History was made in November when the first scheduled flight by an overseas company was made to Luton. Flown by Jetstreams of NetherLines, the service once again connected the airport with Amsterdam to augment those of LEA. Unfortunately, the latter's financial affairs led to the carrier suspending operations in February 1986 pending a reorganisation. Meanwhile the Irish airline, Ryanair, had been granted the licence to fly between Dublin and Luton, starting up in the spring with HS 748s. Such was the popularity of the route that One-Elevens were substituted and the frequencies increased until as many as seven return flights were operated on some days. As the company prospered so its network expanded, until by 1990 routes to Carrickfinn, Cork, Galway, Kerry County, Knock, Shannon, Sligo and Waterford had been added. In the process 1988 had seen a start made to replace the 748s with ATR42s, while a pair of Airbus A320s were ordered for the early 1990s.

At the beginning of 1987 it was announced that the management of Ryanair had acquired LEA, its relaunch set for May. Brussels was the airline's main target for its single One-Eleven, with Amsterdam visited at reduced frequency. The latter service did not prove a success and was quickly withdrawn, but the Belgian link survived until the start of the 1989 summer season when it suffered a similar fate. Over-capacity and timings unsuited to businessmen's requirements were chiefly to blame for the failures. It was therefore decided that LEA would use its solitary aircraft exclusively for charter work or substituting the parent company's aircraft. At the same time the operating name was changed to Ryanair Europe although its base remained at Luton. During 1990 the carrier acquired three of British Island's One-Elevens in order to take over the latter's IT commitments, particularly to Italian destinations.

In mid-1987 Ryanair gained a competitor on the Dublin sector when Virgin Atlantic was awarded the licence. At first a Viscount was leased from British Air Ferries, but in 1988 a pair of Club Air Boeing 727s flew the services for a time before reverting to the BAF machine. In the meantime Virgin had decided to concentrate on its long-haul activities, so Capital successfully applied for the schedule. Once again the Viscount was used initially, but it was a short-term expedient pending the delivery of the first of two BAe 146s in the summer. The Leeds-based airline went on to introduce other regular services into Luton, contributing an impressive amount of traffic to the airport. Sadly the carrier was forced to suspend all operations at the end of June 1990, which left quite a void in the airport's movements.

Ironically, in view of the growing number of domestic passengers, the authorities had decided to construct a separate terminal to help relieve the congestion in the main building. Due to open in early September 1990, only Britannia and Manx provided daily internal schedules at the time. In addition British Midland ensured that there were seasonal links with the Channel Islands, while Monarch offered flights to Malaga, Malta, Menorca and Tenerife several times each week. In the late summer it was expected that Luton-based Air Exel would launch its proposed services with Brussels, Paris and Edinburgh, while in the Netherlands Freeway Air was due to take over the Maastricht run previously maintained by Virgin. In the event neither projects materialised. A further reduction in scheduled traffic was suffered when Ryanair transferred some of its operations to Stansted in the spring of 1991, a loss offset to some extent by several Scandinavian carriers moving from the Essex airport to Luton.

Executive aircraft make considerable use of the airport, often for attention by one of the resident engineering facilities. Mail and parcels traffic during the night is responsible for a large number of regular movements at Luton which is linked with various points around the UK and Europe.

Location and access: Situated southeast of Luton some 2 miles from M1 Junction 10. BR's Luton Flyer runs at frequent intervals throughout the day with an hourly service between midnight and 06.00. It connects Luton with London at St Pancras or King's Cross Thameslink with a journey time of about 45min which includes the coach link between the station and airport. Express coaches are available to most parts of the country, either direct or via London (Victoria), by using route 757. This runs every 30min for most of the day and hourly on Sunday taking about 75min for the trip. Services also operate to Heathrow and Gatwick. Local bus routes connect the town bus station with the airport, while there are express links with Peterborough, Northampton and Milton Keynes

Terminal: The main, northeast-facing international building contains restaurants, bar, buffets and shop. One of the refreshment areas is operated by the Little Chef group with the distinction of being the only one of its kind not parked beside a road. A single-storey domestic terminal is situated at the southeast corner of the site. Facilities include a landside buffet and bar

Spectator facilities: Car park and enclosure are combined alongside the taxiway. No admission charge but a daily flat rate for cars on a 'pay and display' basis. Buffet available in adjacent domestic terminal. Surrounded by a sturdy 10ft-high chain link fence, the facilities are excellent for viewing all movements, but the barrier does make it more difficult to obtain photographs. A wide-angle lens is necessary for aircraft of Boeing 737 size. Mornings are best on sunny days

Operators: Scheduled services by Ryanair (One-Eleven, ATR42), Monarch (Boeing 737/757), British Midland (BAe ATP, DC-9), KLM CityHopper (Fokker 50, Saab 340), Manx Airlines (BAe ATP/146), Air Exel (Brasilia — proposed)

Charter and IT operators: Adria Airways (DC-9), Air Malta (Boeing 737), Alisarda (DC-9), Aviogenex (Boeing 737), Britannia (Boeing 737/757/767), Cyprus Airways (Airbus A310/320), JAT (Boeing 727, DC-9), Kar-Air (Airbus A300, MD-83), Monarch (Boeing 737/757, Airbus A300), London European (One-Eleven), Sterling (Caravelle, Boeing 727), Transwede (MD-80, Boeing 737).

Among the freight operators are Gill Air (Short SD3-30), Channel Express (Herald), Loganair (Short SD3-60), Extra (Beech 99),

Air Bridge (Electra), British Air Ferries (Viscount), TNT (BAe 146), Iona National (Bandeirante), NFD (BAe 146).
Maintenance work by Airline Engineering and Britannia frequently brings in aircraft from other operators. The Luton Flying Club occupies the area on the eastern side of the airport approach road
Movements (1989): Total 73,385 (air

transport 38,247/club 9,644/private 14,342/empty positioning 5,946/test and training 4,799). Total passengers 2,848,244
Runway: 08/26 (7,087ft/2,160m)
Radio frequencies: 119.975MHz (Tower), 129.55MHz, 128.75MHz (Approach), 127.3MHz (Radar)
Telephone: Luton (0582) 405100
Operated by: Luton International Airport Ltd

Lydd

Lydd Airport was built for Silver City in the remarkable short time of seven months to serve as the airline's UK terminal for its car ferry services. Given the appropriate name of Ferryfield, the airport's operational life began on 13 July 1954 with a Freighter flight to Le Touquet. Very soon Deauville and Ostend routes were added, with the result that by the time of its first anniversary, over 34,000 vehicles and 88,000 passengers had passed through the airport.

The impressive figures continued to grow in the fifties and by the sixties other destinations had joined the routes radiating from Lydd, from where over 100 flights per day were quite common in peak periods. However, very gradually competition from the new drive-on/drive-off sea ferries forced a reduction in frequencies, until by the end of 1970 all services had ceased.

Lydd was left without scheduled services apart from the occasional BAe (HS) 748 diverted from fogbound Ashford. The airport was also used for the storage of aircraft awaiting sale, but on 1 November 1974 airline movements were reinstated. Dan-Air's

coach-air service was transferred from Ashford, resulting in the regular appearances of BAe (HS) 748s on the Paris route and seasonal Jersey operations. The cargo airline Air Freight also made the move with its DC-3 fleet, soon after adopting the title of Skyways Cargo Airline. It was not long before most of the previous inhabitants of Ashford followed suit, helping to swell the movements at Lydd considerably.

Dan-Air continued their coach-air service to Beauvais/Paris until the end of the 1970s, whereupon the long established operation finally ended with the winter programme. Similarly the company ceased their summer only Jersey service in October 1979.

Hitherto, Skyways had for many years concentrated on cargo work. In the spring of 1980, the company took over the two Lydd passenger schedules using one of their two FH-227s. It was the first of its type to operate with a UK airline in this role, but proved very satisfactory. Unfortunately in October 1980, the company ceased trading, its fleet sold and dispersed. Lydd was entering another very quiet period, although Dan-Air was still using the airport at night for the purpose of carrying mail to and from Liverpool. This activity also ended in November 1981 when the airport was closed to all traffic.

For a time the future looked bleak, but fortunately the airfield was bought by Hards Travel who reopened it in April 1982. The company was an already established travel operator in the Birmingham area, but wanted to diversify its activities by offering ITs across the Channel using its own airline. Janus Airways was therefore formed equipped with the ex-Brymon Herald in readiness for the inaugural run in December 1982. For the winter an average of four flights on each of five days were planned, followed during the summer by a much expanded timetable calling for some ten daily trips.

The airport's reopening was an event welcomed by those who had mourned its closure. During 1982 an application was successfully made by Instone Air Line to operate a Lydd-Beauvais-Rotterdam-Lydd freight route. A start was made in October the aircraft used being a Bristol Freighter, the type which was responsible for the creation of Lydd in the 1950s. The airline leased a half of the existing hangar for in line maintenance although its headquarters remained at Stansted. Janus Airways occupied the remaining engineering facilities.

In the early part of 1986 the airline was acquired by Euroair which carried on Hards' IT work unchanged. However, it was not long before the tour company was forced to cease trading which meant the end of the coach-air operations. For a time the future of Lydd was once again in jeopardy, but fortunately restricted facilities were continued for the benefit of the many transit light aircraft and local clubs. With new owners in 1987, the airport began to revive although there were still no scheduled or IT flights. A good many improvements were introduced including a modernised passenger terminal and a new executive terminal offering conference facilities if required. A Category 1 instrument landing system was installed on the existing runway, while studies began into the feasibility of a second strip in the future. Lydd's new management began to seek airlines likely to be interested in providing regular services from the airport, particularly those willing to revive the London-Paris route. In 1988 Air Metro was well advanced with its plans to operate schedules from its Bournemouth base to a number of European cities including the French capital and Amsterdam. Each flight was to call at Lydd so it appeared that the latter's prospects looked promising. Unfortunately the CAA did not grant the necessary licences to the new carrier, which was found to be lacking the necessary financial backing. Ellan-Vannin Airlines then took over the troubled company expressing its intention to provide a similar network, but with Jetstreams instead of Metros. Meanwhile, at Lydd the check-in desks already optimistically displayed appropriate information for the expected passengers, which in the event never arrived because EVA also failed to start its promised services.

After these setbacks, hopes were raised again in 1989 when British Independent Airways applied for route licences applicable to the Kent airport. Although the airline was much in evidence during the summer, it did not begin scheduled operations until April 1990 with daily services to Le Touquet with a 748. A Paris link was commenced shortly

afterwards using Beauvais as the French terminal, although it was intended to move to Pontoise as soon as this airfield had received the necessary facilities for commercial work. If BIA is successful in fulfilling its ambitions, then Lydd's fortunes should continue to improve.

As in the case of Manston, a seasonal service to the Channel Islands has been offered through the years with Capital being the latest operator in 1989 and 1990. With the latter's contraction half way through the second season, the flights passed to other carriers as a temporary expedient.

During the summer of 1990 Lydd was one of eight sites suggested for possible major expansion in the quest to satisfy the growth in air transport. Considerable redevelopment would be required before it could play its part and would involve lengthening the runway. One of the main handicaps in its present form is the poor access and ground communications. There has to be a distinct improvement in these if Lydd is to be seriously considered by travellers. BIA obviously acknowledges this because a coach connects with flights to provide a link with London Bridge or the BR station at Ashford.

Location and access: The lengthy airport access road is on the east side of the B2075 some 2 miles from its junction with the A259 near New Romney. Car park charges vary with duration. East Kent bus services from Folkestone bus station take about 75min for the journey, but there is still a long walk to the terminal from the alighting point
Terminal: Single-storey building containing restaurant, bar and buffet
Spectator facilities: None provided. The large clean windows in the buffet look directly on to the apron giving an excellent view of activities. Photographs can also be taken through the glass although reflections are a hazard. A 50mm lens is adequate for a 748 parked immediately in front of the terminal, with afternoons providing the best conditions on sunny days. It is also possible to acquire the occasional photograph through the fence adjacent to the hangar or along the access road
Operators: Scheduled services by British Independent Airways (BAe 748)
Charter and IT operator: Varies year to year. Club and privately-owned aircraft contribute most of the movements
Movements (1989): Total 44,932 (air

transport 484/club 19,140/private 12,687/test and training 9,250). Total passengers 2,962
Runway: 04/22 (4,934ft/1,504m)

Radio frequencies: 120.7MHz (Tower and Approach)/131.3MHz (Radar)
Telephone: Lydd (0679) 20401
Owned by: Lydd Airport Group Ltd

Manchester (Ringway)

Ringway was opened on 25 June 1938 to replace the inadequate airport at Barton. Domestic and international services were developed by Railway Air Services, Isle of Man Services and KLM. The airfield also had on site the presence of Fairey Aviation and Avro, both engaged in the assembly and test flying of aircraft for the RAF. Operationally Ringway was used only briefly by various units employed in the defence of Manchester, its main claim to fame during the war was its role as home for the Central Landing School formed in 1940. This unit was created to train paratroops, saboteurs and members of raiding parties from the lessons learned from the Germans in Europe.

The increasing use of the airfield resulted in hard runways being laid in 1941, followed soon after by a split in the responsibilities of the School. The Glider element was posted to Sherburn in Yorkshire, while Ringway remained the base for the newly created No

1 Parachute Training School until March 1946.

It was June 1946 before commercial flying restarted, the first scheduled service being flown by Air France on the Paris route. Later that year Ringway became the home of No 613 Squadron which then remained until it disbanded in 1957. In the mid-1950s the need to expand the airport facilities was apparent, resulting in a massive programme of reconstruction starting in 1957. Five years later the new terminal building was officially opened which brought the airport up to a very high standard.

The advent of the wide bodied airliners necessitated further development in the 1970s, when a new complex for international flights was provided plus additional car parks and approach roads. Manchester is now the largest UK airport outside London with services to most centres in Europe. It is also the terminal for North American, African, Middle and Far East scheduled services while numerous passenger and cargo charters are operated by a variety of carriers both UK and foreign. A shuttle service to London using One-Elevens and Tridents was started in the autumn of 1979 by British Airways, these types later replaced by the Boeing 757.

The One-Elevens of British Airways are looked after at the carrier's facility on the airport, while Dan-Air's engineering presence takes care of the airline's 748s and One-Elevens plus those of other operators as required.

Internal improvements to the terminal began in 1982, providing new style buffets, restaurant, coffee bar and expanded shopping area. Outside, rearrangements of the terminal access roads were designed to give additional parking spaces and a new bus/coach station. Enlargement of the western apron provided sufficient parking space for four Boeing 747s, while in February 1984 work began on the extension to the international Pier C. Other improvements continued to be implemented, but the next major change scheduled was the construction of a brand new terminal exclusively for the use of domestic passengers. Costing £27 million it was opened in the spring of 1989 to replace Pier A built in 1962. Although completely self-contained with its own restaurant, shops and multi-storey car park, there is a linkway with the main concourse for the benefit of transfer passengers.

While the new structure was intended to handle 2.5 million passengers annually, in the long-term even greater expansion was needed. In April 1988 approval was given for the provision of a brand new terminal to be built for use in the mid-1990s. Situated to the northwest of the present complex, the site was already owned by the airport although the diversion of a local road will be necessary. An interesting design was selected which makes use of a fairly shallow two-storey building on the edge of the apron. This main concourse will be flanked by long fingers along which the various gates will be positioned. Parallel, but some distance in front of the principal structure, will be a remote island pier reached by means of two underground passageways. It is expected that phase one will be ready to assist with the anticipated 12 million passengers using Manchester in 1992, a total forecast to rise to 20 million by the end of the decade. No doubt many will use the new airport rail station due to open in the early 1990s, which will provide a direct link with the northern BR network and give a speedy service into the city.

Location and access: Situated 10 miles south of Manchester, directly connected to the M56 at Junction 5. Large car parks, both multi-storey and surface, although the latter are for long-term stays. For short periods the multi-storey is satisfactory but the restricted height of 2m produces parking problems for vehicles over this figure. Charges are graduated. Bus services 44, 300 and 369 include the nearest rail station at Heald Green in their travels, the 44 going on to the city centre which it reaches one hour after leaving the airport. A 4-mile journey takes the 300 to Wilmslow BR station which is on the London-Manchester main line. Express coach route 757 runs every 30min from Manchester Victoria and Chorlton Street coach station, trimming the elapsed time for the trip to 20min

Terminal: Large modern building containing restaurant, buffet, bar and various shops. The first floor concourse displays a glass screen commemorating the 60,000 paratroops trained at Ringway, a memorial to Alcock and Brown and four enormous Venetian chandeliers suspended from the roof each weighing two tons. The domestic terminal has its own refreshment facilities

Spectator facilities: During the years much of the roof terrace has been withdrawn from use as the terminal building has been expanded. Now only the section along the front of the main building remains available which is reached via an external stairway. From this vantage point most movements can be seen although the area tends to become crowded with spectators. Photographs are not easy to obtain because of the narrow field of vision and a 200mm lens is necessary for most types as they taxi past the end of the piers. There is no longer a charge for entrance. An enthusiast's shop is open daily on the terrace selling all essential reading matter, models and other items

Operators: Scheduled services by Aberdeen Airways (Gulfstream 1), Aer Lingus (Boeing 737, Fokker 50), Aeroflot (Tu-154), Air Canada (TriStar, Boeing 767), Air France (Boeing 737, Fellowship, Airbus A320), Air Hong Kong (Boeing 707-freight), Air Kilroe (Jetstream), Air Littoral (Brasilia), Air Malta (Boeing 737), Air Portugal (Boeing 737), Alitalia (DC-9), American Airlines (Boeing 767), British Airways (Boeing 747/757, TriStar, One-Eleven, BAe ATP/748), Business Air (Saab SF340), Canadian Airlines International (Boeing 767), Cathay Pacific (Boeing 747), Cyprus Airways (Airbus A310/320), Dan-Air (BAe

146, One-Eleven), El Al (Boeing 757), Emery Worldwide (DC-8-freight), Emirates (Airbus A310), Finnair (Boeing 737-freight), GB Air (Boeing 737), Gill Air (Short SD3-30), Iberia (DC-9, MD-80), JAT (DC-9, Boeing 727/737), Jersey European (Friendship), KLM (Boeing 737, Airbus A310), Loganair (Short SD3-60, BAe 146/ATP), LOT (Tu-154), Lufthansa (Boeing 737), Manx Airlines (Short SD3-60/BAe ATP), Qantas (Boeing 747), Pakistan International (Boeing 747), Ryanair (One-Eleven, ATR-42), Sabena (Boeing 737), SAS (DC-9), Singapore Airways (Boeing 747), South African Airways (Boeing 747), Suckling Airways (Dornier Do228), Swissair (Airbus A310)

Charter and IT operators: Adria Airways (MD-80, DC-9, Airbus A320), Air Atlantis (Boeing 737), Air Columbus (Boeing 737), Air Europa (Boeing 737/757), Air Europe (Boeing 737/757), Air Malta (Boeing 737), Airtours (MD-83), Air Transat (TriStar), Air UK (BAe 146), Air UK Leisure (Boeing 737), Air 2000 (Boeing 757), American Trans Air (TriStar, Boeing 757), Aviogenex (Boeing 727/737), Balkan (Tu-154), Birmingham European (One-Eleven), Britannia (Boeing 737/757/767), Caledonian Airways (Boeing 757, TriStar), Cyprus Airways (Airbus A310), Dan-Air (Boeing 727/737, One-Eleven), Futura Airways (Boeing 737), Inter European (Boeing 737), LOT (IL-18, Tu-134/154), Monarch (Boeing 737/757), Noble Air (Boeing 727), Nortjet (Boeing 737), Oasis (MD-80), Royal Air Maroc (Boeing 727), Spanair (MD-80), Tarom (One-Eleven), Trans European (Boeing 737), Viva Air (Boeing 737), Worldways (DC-8, TriStar).

A number of company, club and privately-owned aircraft are based at the airport (south side)

Movements (1989): Total 155,215 (air transport 121,140/private 8,483/club 12,145). Total passengers 10,392,733
Runway: 06/24 (10,000ft/3,048m)
Radio frequencies: 118.625MHz (Tower)/ 119.4MHz (Approach)/ 121.35MHz (Radar)
Telephone: 061-489 3000
Owned by: Manchester International Airport PLC

Newcastle (Woolsington)

Passenger services began at the newly opened airport in 1935 when North Eastern Airways introduced routes to Edinburgh and London. Domestic routes were further developed up until the war, whereupon civil flying was suspended. Although requisitioned and used by the Air Ministry, Woolsington did not benefit from any development as in the majority of similar cases.

When commercial flying restarted, Newcastle did not regain its original routes immediately. In 1948 only a summer Isle of Man service was flown by Northern Air Charter, although the following year saw greater expansion with Lancashire Aircraft Corporation who set up a base at the airport. Operations had passed into the hands of Hunting by 1953, but before regular Dakota services could be flown, the airport had to be modernised. Several international routes were introduced bringing the airline's schedules in mid-1954 to 35 per week.

In response to this visible growth the airport authorities agreed to a programme of expansion to permit operation of the brand new Viscounts then entering service. In 1955 the type was introduced on various Hunting routes out of Newcastle using the newly provided runway. However, despite these developments, passenger figures remained unimpressive, which resulted in the airline withdrawing after two and a half years of effort.

Other airlines continued to offer a few services, but BKS eventually became the major operator, restarting the London route in 1959. Subsequently the airline expanded its route network, eventually changing its name to Northeast to reflect its association with the region. Until its absorption into British Airways in 1976 the carrier played a big part in the development of air transport at Newcastle.

The airport is now connected to London not only by the flag carrier, but also by Dan-Air who provides a Gatwick alternative in addition to serving Jersey and Amsterdam. The Dutch city is also served by Air UK, and the airline expects to restore a Stansted link in 1991. Locally-based Gill Air has steadily increased its scheduled work with its collection of SD3-30s to include Aberdeen, Belfast City and Manchester in its regular coverage. A new domestic service was launched by Birmingham European in 1989 to enable passengers to connect with European flights at the Midlands airport. This quickly proved very popular, with the result that the Gulfstream 1 employed needed to be replaced by an SD3-60.

This expansion was assisted in no small way by the considerable development undertaken at the airport in 1966/67. At this time a new terminal complex was constructed in addition to runway and taxiway improvements. Further work was carried out on the terminal in 1981/82 which created more space for passenger reception, baggage handling, waiting areas, etc, while the pier modernisation programme greatly improved the access to aircraft by passengers. Later in the 1980s the provision of a taxiway parallel to the runway removed any problems with congestion due to back-tracking.

Although the number of movements has steadily risen, the lack of suitable accommodation has not encouraged the handling of cargo on a large scale. With this in mind, in mid-1990 the authorities announced that they proposed to build a freight complex to the south of the terminal. If planning permission is forthcoming without undue delay, then work should start in 1991 for completion during the following year.

Location and access: Situated 6 miles northwest of Newcastle on A696. Car park charges graduated. Central rail station is directly linked to the airport by Blue Bus Services X77 which runs half-hourly with a journey time of 25min. Other services by this company operate from Eldon Square Bus Concourse and pass the airport entrance en route to their various destinations. Alternatively route M77 is an Air Link bus which runs every 10min between the airport and the Metro station at Kenton Bank Foot. Onward travel can then be made by the Metro system either to central or other parts of the northeast

Terminal: Three-storey building contains restaurant, bar, lounge areas, shop and buffet. Prices charged in the latter are expensive so it is worthwhile patronising the drinks vending machine located in the shop on the ground floor

Spectator facilities: A roof terrace open throughout the year gives an excellent view of all movements. Entrance is via internal stairs, admission free. A buffet is available in busy periods during the summer. Also an excellent vantage point for photographs, although a telephoto lens is necessary in most cases. Late mornings and afternoons are best in sunny conditions. The waiting area within the building is also a good observation point and is much warmer than the east-facing roof. Double glazing does not help photography

Operators: Scheduled services by Aer Lingus (Short SD3-60), Air France/TAT (Fellowship), Air UK (BAe 146), Birmingham European (Gulfstream 1, Short SD3-60), British Airways (One-Eleven, Boeing

737/757, Airbus A320), Brymon Airways (Dash Seven), Dan-Air (One-Eleven, BAe 146), Gill Air (Short SD3-30), Manx Airlines (Short SD3-60), Sabena/Delta Air Transport (Brasilia)

Charter and IT operators: Adria Airways (DC-9), Aeroflot (Tu-154), Air Atlantis (Boeing 737), Air Europa (Boeing 737), Air Malta (Boeing 737), Air UK Leisure (Boeing 737), Air 2000 (Boeing 757), American Trans Air (Boeing 757), Aviogenex (Boeing 737), Balkan (Tu-154), Britannia (Boeing 737), Brymon Airways (Dash Seven), Cyprus Airways (Airbus A310), Dan-Air

(Boeing 727/737, One-Eleven), JAT (DC-9), Monarch Airlines (Boeing 737), Oasis (MD-80), Royal Air Maroc (Boeing 737), Spanair (MD-80), Worldways (DC-8, TriStar)

Movements (1989): Total 57,485 (air transport 24,912/club 16,484/private 11,150). Total passengers 1,570,218

Runway: 07/25 (7,651ft/2,332m)

Radio frequencies: 119.7MHz (Tower)/126.35MHz (Approach)/ 118.5MHz (Radar)

Telephone: Newcastle (091) 2860966

Operated by: Newcastle International Airport Ltd

Newquay (St Mawgan)

Although built for the use of Coastal Command during the war, a small part of the site had been used for a time prewar by the first scheduled passenger services to Newquay. In 1947 the airfield was run down by the RAF, but for a few years seasonal civil operations were able to continue. A change of policy by 1951 found St Mawgan earmarked for development as the main Coastal Command base in the southwest, preventing any further airline traffic until 1959.

Services were then established to Liverpool and Glasgow by Starways, with routes to London and the Scillies added by Westpoint and Mayflower by 1963. About this time it was found necessary to provide improved terminal facilities, a small building being opened on 22 May 1965.

Newquay has seen a wide variety of aircraft types operated by a selection of carriers since the early days. At one point One-Elevens were used on the London service by British Eagle, but after the airline's demise in 1968, Dan-Air Dakotas and

Ambassadors took over until British Midland became the licence holder. The company employed Viscounts and Heralds for this moderately patronised service, but the airline slowly built it up to give satisfactory returns.

Rationalisation of routes found Brymon taking the route over in early 1977, at the same time assuming responsibility for the running of the airport facility. A Herald was acquired for use on the London service, although it was also employed on Aberdeen and Manchester schedules in between its normal duties or at weekends. This aircraft (G-ATIG) was replaced on the service in November 1982 when one of Brymon's new Dash Sevens took over the responsibility. The type steadily improved the loads carried until four return flights each weekday were justified with a reduced frequency at weekends. In the mid-1980s the airline also introduced a seasonal link with the Isles of Scilly and Bristol which necessitated the use of a Twin Otter. By 1989 only one example of the type remained with the carrier, specifically for use on the sectors to St Mary's from Plymouth and Exeter. This kept the machine fully employed so the direct Newquay run was dropped, although it is possible that the service may be reinstated in the future following a decision to extend the island airport's runway.

In the past other attempts have been made to provide the area with regular flights but with little success. A new route was introduced in 1978 by Air Anglia, connecting St Mawgan with Swansea, Birmingham and Norwich. Like the Brymon service, it was aimed particularly at businessmen since no longer is Newquay purely a holiday only airport. However, the route did not prove to be an economic proposition and was removed from the network after the 1979 season. In 1982 the Liverpool based airline Genair

introduced a weekend service from Merseyside using a Bandeirante. Loads were not exceptional and since the route did not play a major part in the company's future plans, it was soon dropped.

Apart from the scheduled movements, a number of executive aircraft are regular visitors. It also remains a very active RAF base for Nimrods as well as hosting numerous visiting military aircraft from many air forces.

Location and access: Situated 5 miles northeast of Newquay off B3276. No charge for short stay car parking. A Western National bus route from Newquay passes the terminal
Terminal: Small single storey building containing lounge and snack bar which is normally open at times of scheduled movements
Spectator facilities: Viewing possible from small area in front of terminal or from adjacent car park. Reasonable for photography, although on sunny days conditions become more difficult particularly in the afternoon.
After the last departure at midday on Saturday the entire complex is closed and locked until it is time for the Sunday evening flights
Operators: Scheduled services by Brymon Airways (Dash Seven, Dash Eight). Charters mainly by company executive types
Movements (1990): Figures not reported
Runway: 13/31 (9,000ft/2,743m). It is a Master Diversion Aerodrome
Radio frequencies: 123.4MHz (Tower)/126.5MHz (Approach)/125.55MHz (Radar)
Telephone: St Mawgan (0637) 860551
Operated by: Brymon Airports Ltd (Civil). Ministry of Defence airfield

Norwich (Horsham St Faith)

Horsham was built prewar but did not become fully operational until June 1940 although detachments of several squadrons were based for short spells prior to this date. The Blenheim IV-equipped Nos 139 and 114 Squadrons were the first full time residents, but the latter's stay was of short duration. The airfield became the home of the first operational Mosquitos, No 105

Squadron taking the type on its inaugural mission on 31 May 1942.

Horsham was offered to the USAAF in late 1942, resulting in the arrival of the 319th Bomb Group with B-26 Marauders. By early 1943, P-47 Thunderbolts of the 56th Fighter Group had replaced the bombers, but soon moved on in order to permit work to commence on runway construction. On completion the airfield was suitable for heavy bomber use, thereafter becoming the base of the 458th Bomb Group which arrived in January 1944 equipped with B-24

Liberators. From the first on 24 February 1944 until the final raid on 25 April 1945, the Group flew 240 missions from Horsham, dropping over 13,000 tons of bombs in the process.

After the Americans left in July 1945, the airfield reverted to RAF control. The Mosquito reappeared for a time, but the main type to use Horsham was the Meteor. The longest stay was by No 74 Squadron which remained for 13 years, 11 of them with this type. From 1956 until the end of the decade, Javelins of No 23 Squadron shared the base with Hunters, but by mid-1960 all the fighters had left. During the 1940s and 1950s the station was also regularly used by the auxiliary squadrons for their summer camps.

Plans to adapt the airfield into a civil airport for Norwich were well advanced in the early sixties, but it was not until 30 May 1970 that it was officially opened. Before this the runways had been fully renovated, landing aids installed and passenger handling facilities provided for the token services operated by Channel Airways. Norwich became the headquarters of Air Anglia, a newly formed airline which aimed to provide scheduled services for East Anglia.

The routes and fleet gradually expanded until at the time of the formation of Air UK, the network took in Aberdeen, Amsterdam, Birmingham, Heathrow, Humberside, Jersey, Leeds, Newcastle, Stansted, Stavanger and Teesside non stop. In addition Bergen, Edinburgh, Glasgow, Newquay and Swansea were all served via one or two intermediate stops. This considerable traffic increase at Norwich had tended to outgrow the terminal facilities. In 1976/77 over 155,000 passengers used the airport, some 26% in excess of the recognised capacity of the building. By 1977/78 the figure had risen to 182,000, causing urgent consideration to be given to improving the existing facilities pending the provision of a new terminal, a project which could take ten years.

However, the pressure was relieved in 1980 by the steady cut backs introduced by Air UK. By the summer of 1982, the network covered direct links with Amsterdam, Edinburgh, Jersey, Leeds and Teesside with Aberdeen, Bergen and Stavanger reached after one or two stops. Frequencies too were much reduced with the exception of the Dutch services which have always been the most popular.

The licences previously held by Air UK involving Humberside and London were taken up by Eastern Airways. The Heathrow route was at first flown with a DC-3, which served a useful purpose in gaining publicity. Thereafter a Short SD3-30 was the standard equipment. The airline introduced an alternative London destination in 1982 when a Gatwick link was started. It was arranged to connect with the Humberside SD3-30, giving the Lincolnshire passengers the option of either London airport. The popularity of the service was such that an SD3-60 was substituted on some timings, a proportion of which by-passed Norwich.

In the autumn of 1982, Eastern merged with Genair and Casair to provide a more economic operation. The effect on Norwich was to increase the routes flown to include Birmingham, Liverpool and later Esbjerg, elevating the carrier to the position of the major operator at the airport. It was a situation destined to be short-lived. In June 1984 Genair ceased trading leaving Air UK as the sole provider of scheduled services from the Norfolk airport once again, the newly vacated routes becoming the target for several interested carriers. Successful in its application for the Humberside-Norwich-Heathrow link, Air UK was able to restore the sectors to its network after a couple of years or so with Genair. Otherwise the services on offer by the airline remained largely unchanged, although in 1987 a daily return flight to Frankfurt was added, the Friendship staging via Stansted in both directions. Newcomer Holland Aero Lines introduced a route to Rotterdam in early 1985, but the Nomad-maintained operation was suspended at the end of the following year.

Following this brief interlude Air UK once again became the sole provider of schedules, although when the carrier decided to drop the Heathrow link at the end of the 1989/90 winter programme due to poor loads and increasing costs, some interest was shown by Navco Airways.

The engineering centre originally set up by Air Anglia continues to carry out maintenance and overhauls not only on Air UK Friendships, but also on those of the species belonging to other airlines around the world. All of this work had been carried out in the ex-RAF hangars which, although adequate for the turboprops, were not suitable for the new fleet additions. With the arrival of the 146s something larger was required, so a new jet base was financed by the airport authorities and built to the airline's specification. Occupation began in February 1990, the single-span building offering nearly 30,000sq ft of floor space and the ability to accommodate three 146s or two 737-400s side-by-side. Norwich is also used for the open storage of Heralds and Friendships awaiting new operators.

A new cargo centre was opened in August 1978 which offered greater opportunities for expansion into the freight market. Norwich was an early participant in the Post Office's nightly mail flights, the contracts regularly changing hands but usually calling for the use of either Bandeirantes, Titans, Twin Otters or similar aircraft.

After many years in the pending file, the plans for a brand new terminal were finally dusted off in 1987 for a start to be made on its construction. Originally expected to be located on the northern perimeter, problems in the planning stages dictated that it was positioned in the southwestern corner instead. At least this was nearer to the city and allowed direct access to the main road. Opened in 1988, the replacement building is a single-storey structure of modern design which could be mistaken at first glance for a low-level DIY warehouse. Nevertheless it is practical and adequate for Norwich's needs.

Location and access: Situated 3 miles north of Norwich some 200m beyond the junction of the A140 Cromer Road and Fifers Lane. Car park charges graduated. Eastern Counties City Line bus route 11 connects the airport terminal with the city centre at 20min intervals. The entrance in Fifers Lane still gives access to the Air UK engineering facility

Terminal: A modern single-storey building containing bar, buffet, shop and restaurant

Spectator facilities: A grass viewing area with picnic tables is provided at the western end of the terminal. Since this is alongside the taxiway it is a good vantage point for observing all movements. Unfortunately the 6ft fence is not photographer friendly, although the difficulties can be overcome. A 200mm lens is necessary for smaller subjects on the apron, but a 50mm is sufficient for taxiway shots although in this case it is not possible to focus the mesh out of the frame. Some extra height is therefore required to obtain a clear shot. Use of the tables for such a purpose is, quite rightly, discouraged, but alternative means of temporary elevation can be found

Operators: Scheduled services by Air UK (Friendship, Short SD3-60, BAe 146), Navco Airways (Dornier 228) in prospect
Charter and IT operators: Aviogenex (Boeing 727/737), Britannia (Boeing 737). Numerous company and privately owned aircraft are to be seen, both visiting and resident

Movements (1989): Total 33,867 (air transport 10,674/private 5,810/test and training 15,278). Total passengers 225,329
Runway: 09/27 (6,043ft/1,842m)

Radio frequencies: 118.9MHz (Tower)/119.35MHz (Approach)
Telephone: Norwich (0603) 425251
Operated by: Norwich Airport Ltd

Penzance

Penzance Heliport became the mainland terminal for BEA's Scilly Islands service on 1 September 1964. Earlier that year the fixed wing Rapides had been replaced by one of the new Sikorsky S-61Ns, although the helicopter continued to use Lands End (St Just) until the new heliport was completed.

It became the first fully equipped terminal of its kind in the UK, capable of handling passengers and freight plus having the facility for in-line maintenance work in a small hangar. The British Airways Helicopters' operation was carried out with one S-61N, the aircraft relieved by another of the type when major overhauls were due. After the sale of the airline this arrangement was continued by what is now known as British International Helicopters.

There was little apparent change in the operations with Saturdays continuing to be the busiest day for the services and Sunday still a day of rest due to the airport at St Mary's being closed. Obviously the holiday season provides a peak in the movements graph, with the S-61 shuttling backwards and forwards on its 50min return trip, the

minimum time being spent in the turnround. Since taking over, BIH has maintained the schedules with very few alterations including the continuation of the sector to Tresco introduced by the previous operator in 1983. Objections were vigorously made against an application for a competitive route from Land's End/St Just, but on the second attempt Isles of Scilly Skybus were granted the licence for start-up in the spring of 1987. Fares were slightly below those of BIH, expecially the popular day return. Despite all fears the newcomer's presence had little detrimental effect upon the helicopter operation, with ample traffic supporting both modes of transport. In fact frequencies have subsequently been increased to both St Mary's and Tresco during the summer months.

Additional movements at Penzance have been generated by the need to support the rigs off the southwest coast, and the regular visits by the helicopters used by Trinity House to service the local lighthouses.

Location and access: Situated just under 1 mile east of Penzance on the A30. Car park has graduated charges. A coach service connects the flights with the BR

81

Above:
Although a much smaller area than in the past, Heathrow's roof terrace still gives opportunities for photographs either of aircraft using the near stands or of those on the taxiways. Lufthansa's A320 D-AIPN is a relatively new addition to the regulars. *AJW*

Below:
Considerable traffic is generated at Humberside by the oil support work undertaken by Bond Helicopters. Sikorsky S-76A G-CBJB is one of a number so employed. *AJW*

Bottom:
Isles of Scilly Skybus Islander G-AXWP departs from St Just on another quick sortie to the islands. *AJW*

Above:
Wearing Air France's livery and titles, Dash Seven G-BRYA departs from London City on a service to Strasbourg. *AJW*

Below:
Boeing 707s are usually to be found at Manston while undergoing some form of overhaul or conversion. Turkish newcomer Golden Horn acquired TC-GHB for freight work in 1990. *AJW*

Bottom:
This Newcastle roof-top shot of Gill Air's Short SD3-30 G-BIYG serves to illustrate the fairly basic livery adopted by the company. *AJW*

station while a number of buses regularly pass the heliport to and from Penzance bus station

Terminal: The small building contains a bar, buffet and waiting area

Spectator facilities: Viewing is satisfactory from the terminal area or over the perimeter fence bordering the main road, although in the late 1980s the latter became dual carriageway thereby reducing the grass verge. Photographs from this vantage point are easy to obtain using a 135mm lens although the new fence is closely boarded and 6ft high. Fortunately it is not difficult to locate an object to provide the necessary additional height. At least if a shot is missed there is usually a second chance in under an hour. During the summer BIH operates scenic local flights on Tuesdays and Thursdays between 12.30 and 14.00 with a choice of a 7min trip round the bay or a 20min excursion taking in Land's End

Operators: Scheduled services by British International Helicopters (Sikorsky S-61N). Regular visits by BIH (Westland WG-30), Trinity House (Bolkow Bo105) and others

Movements (1989): Total 5,353 (air transport 4,690/test and training 126). Total passengers 92,309

Runway: Landing pad 100ft×100ft (30m×30m) with a grass manoeuvring area 09/27 (1,240ft/378m) parallel with the A30

Radio frequency: 118.1MHz

Telephone: Penzance (0736) 64296

Operated by: British International Helicopters Ltd

Plymouth City

Originally a polo field, the site at Roborough hosted an air service as early as 1923 when a route linking the city with Birmingham, Manchester and Belfast was introduced. It was a little too ambitious for the period so the service was soon ended, the field returning to its more familiar role. At the end of the decade the same land was chosen once again for the use of flying machines, but this time it was to play the part of Plymouth's civic aerodrome. Arriving in the Westland Wessex demonstrator G-ABEG, the Prince of Wales officially opened the facility on 15 July 1931, although it was the local aero club that provided most of the activity until the Great Western Railway took a cautious interest in air services. Imperial Airways began operating between Cardiff, Torquay and Plymouth on behalf of the company in the summer of 1933, later extending the route to Birmingham. As a result of this experiment Railway Air Services was formed, its first route linking Plymouth and Liverpool via Teignmouth, Cardiff and Birmingham. Great Western & Southern took over some of the operations in 1938, including the Plymouth network which by now covered the Scillies. A London flight was also offered, although this routed via the south coast airfields on its unhurried journey to the capital.

Used by the RAF occasionally before the war, in 1939 all civil flying was stopped and the airfield requisitioned by the Admiralty. Communication flights were numerous, while target towing aircraft worked with the Devonport gunnery school. During the summer of 1940 the Gladiator-equipped No 247 Squadron reformed at Roborough in readiness for the daytime defence of the city. A detachment was stationed at nearby St Eval for night operations. With Hurricanes replacing the elderly biplanes at the end of the year, the airfield was really not entirely suitable for the unit, so when the opportunity presented itself a move was made to Portreath. Target towing and communications work then continued with a motley collection of types throughout the war until civil flying was resumed in 1946.

Subsequently Plymouth received the attentions of a number of airlines, all offering services to many of the traditional destinations such as the Scillies and Channel Islands. Dan-Air at one time operated a route to Newcastle via Bristol, Cardiff and Liverpool, but the Plymouth sector was later removed from the schedules. London has also been served both direct and via Exeter using a variety of types, but the physical dimensions of the airport always controlled the size of airliner employed and therefore the economics of the operations.

Since 1975 Plymouth has been operated by Brymon Airways, an airline which had started scheduled services three years earlier with an Islander. Its route network steadily expanded to take in Jersey, Guernsey, Cork, the Scillies, Newquay, Aberdeen, Gatwick, Heathrow and London City. Until Brymon took control, the small airfield was grass-covered, a description which gradually became more and more inaccurate under the scorching sun of 1975. It hastened the decision to lay 2,500ft of runway 06/24 with tarmac, followed five years later by a similar treatment for the second runway. Larger airliners could then be handled with greater ease, providing of course that they were able to accept the length limitations.

Brymon used Twin Otters alongside the Islanders from 1974, but in 1979 the last of the latter type left the fleet. In August 1981 the first of the company's Dash Sevens was received and early in the next year the type began to operate the daily Plymouth-Heathrow service. Later many of the Channel Islands timings were taken over by the larger machine, although the Gatwick and Scillies sectors remained a Twin Otter preserve for some years. Survival has never been easy for airlines in the southwest, so it was not surprising that in the early 1980s some reorganisation became necessary if there was to be a future. The new management succeeded in transforming the ailing company into a profitable airline by 1986, attracting the attentions of business travellers to the area by providing convenient flights to and from the capital.

Plymouth became a model for the new London City STOLport during the outline planning proceedings, each having a runway of similar dimensions. Brymon was involved in the new project from the beginning, using its experiences at its home base to reinforce its claim to route licences when the time arrived. On 22 July 1987 the airline duly commissioned the world's first city-centre, international airport, a status reached by the West Country site following extensive development at a cost of over £3 million. A runway of increased length and equipped with modern lighting and landing aids opened the way for a variety of new-generation regional airliners to serve Plymouth, now marketed as a Cityclass airport by the operator.

Military aviation still flourished at the airfield, remaining the base of the Britannia Royal Naval College Air Experience Flight. This Airwork-operated unit was formed in early 1961 to provide some means of pilot selection for the FAA. Initially Tiger Moths wers used, but in 1966 Chipmunks took over the duties, a type which remains the equipment after more than 20 years.

Location and access: Situated 5 miles along Plymbridge Lane which is reached via Derriford Road from the A386, 4 miles north of Plymouth. Well signposted. Car park charges graduated with a short free period. Plymouth Citybus, City Shuttle and Western National services pass the access road at regular intervals to and from the city centre
Terminal: An attractive single-storey building completed in 1982 contains lounge area and snack bar, both of which overlook the apron

Spectator facilities: None provided, but viewing is possible from within the terminal. Photographs can be obtained through the glass with care. The erection of new buildings alongside the terminal has filled gaps which originally offered vantage points, leaving only limited opportunities in the area. Good landing shots can be secured at the threshold of runway 24, although unfortunately the erection of a 10ft-high security fence in 1987 has introduced difficulties when attempting to photograph aircraft taxying prior to take-off

Operators: Scheduled services by Brymon Airways (Dash Seven, Dash Eight). Regular visits by executive types in addition to club and private aircraft
Movement (1989): 36,275 (air transport 7,118/private 3,141/military 24,037). Total passengers 145,090
Runways: 06/24 (2,467ft/752m) 13/31 (3,905ft/1,190m)
Radio frequencies: 122.6MHz (Tower)/133.55MHz (Approach)
Telephone: Plymouth (0752) 705151
Operated by: Plymouth City Airport Ltd

Prestwick

The mid-1930s saw many fields set aside for flying, one near the village of Monkton in Ayrshire opening in 1935. The Duke of Hamilton and the late Gp Capt Duncan McIntyre formed Scottish Aviation on the site, the company becoming responsible for the Tiger Moths of 12 EFTS and later the Ansons of 1 Air Observer Navigation School.

Known as an RAF station in 1939, it became a transit centre for many squadrons in addition to maintaining its training role. Scottish Aviation also steadily built up its repair and overhaul facility, but Prestwick's main claim to fame came with its use as the base for the North Atlantic ferry operations.

Thousands of American and Canadian built aircraft staged through on delivery to the Allied forces, while 8th and 9th USAAF groups often made their first European landings at Prestwick. It was a remarkable station with a mixture of civilian and service personnel. Scottish Aviation retained much of the responsibility for the day to day organisation, controlling all catering, motor transport and works services. It was an obvious choice for a postwar airport.

It became second in importance to Heathrow immediately after the war, with various carriers including the airport in their schedules. Much rivalry has always existed between the Glasgow airports and Prestwick, but the latter remained the Scottish international terminal probably assisted by its excellent weather record. It even became the headquarters for a new company in 1987 when Highland Express began operations with a single Boeing 747. The aircraft became a regular sight as it staged through the airport on its way to New York, or Stansted and Birmingham on the inbound sectors. Unfortunately its timekeeping suffered every time the 747 displayed one of its frequent technical defects which did nothing to help the carrier's image. With costs escalating and still crippled by the expenses incurred at the launch, the airline was forced to cease trading at the end of the year.

In the meantime Glasgow was preparing for a major expansion which would at last make it feasible for long haul movements to be handled. Long before the new enlarged facilities were completed, pressure exerted by such as Air 2000 persuaded the authorities to allow the airline to operate its transatlantic charters from Glasgow in 1990. Not surprisingly it was not long before the scheduled operators had followed suit which, of course, only added to the general congestion.

Passengers accustomed to Prestwick's spaciousness quickly noted the change because now there were domestic plus European scheduled and IT travellers in the terminal. Such traffic had always been very limited at the Ayrshire airport due to the undoubted convenient location of its neighbour. Not all airlines transferred their activities, but how long they will remain at Prestwick after the Glasgow modernisation programme is completed remains to be seen.

At least there has been an increase in the number of cargo flights in recent times. Many of these are in connection with the overnight movement of parcels and packages brought in by such as Federal Express and United Parcels. These are then resorted for onward travel on the shorter sectors to European centres. This business should therefore ensure the survival of the airport because there seems little to be gained by following the example of the passenger airlines. After all, it will then still be available to accept diversions when the weather in the Clyde valley is less than hospitable.

Apart from commercial movements, the airport has seen Scottish Aviation produce the Pioneer and Twin Pioneer in the fifties, while the Bulldog and military Jetstream flowed from the production line in the seventies. Now as a part of British Aerospace, the Scottish division is concentrating on the production and sales of the Jetstream which has enjoyed considerable success in the US. In the late 1980s BAe opened a flying training college equipped with a fleet of Warriors and Senecas. Much overhaul and repair work has been carried out for military forces, particularly the RCAF and later CAF. In the postwar years Scottish Aviation had also operated its own airline on both scheduled and charter work, but commercial flying ended in November 1960 mainly as a result of the termination of trooping contracts.

For many years the USAF maintained its own base at Prestwick, not only handling the numerous transit flights, but also its air-sea rescue unit. After closing down the American facility, the site became HMS Gannet on 23 November 1971 for the use of No 819 Squadron's Sea Kings.

Location and access: Situated some 30 miles south of Glasgow via the A77 to a point about 7 miles south of Kilmarnock. The A78 and A79 lead to the airport, the route being well signposted from central Glasgow. Car parks have graduated charges. Scottish Citylink coaches connect with scheduled flight arrivals and departures by running between the airport and Glasgow (Buchanan Street bus station). A similar service operates to Edinburgh (St Andrews bus station). Bearing in mind the scarcity of scheduled flights use of the half-hourly Western SMT service to Ayr via the airport is more reliable. It runs from Anderson Cross and Buchanan Street bus stations. Service 501 links Edinburgh with Ayr also including the airport in its journey. Trains run every 30min between Glasgow (Central) and Prestwick railway stations, the latter being about one mile from the airport to which it is linked by a courtesy coach at times coinciding with airliner movements
Terminal: Contains buffet, bar, restaurant, shop and large spacious lounge areas
Spectator facilities: A terrace is provided on the second floor overlooking the apron and runway. There is no charge for admission. Excellent views are afforded of all movements, while it is also possible to obtain good photographs, although this is normally with the assistance of a telephoto lens. Lighting conditions are favourable for most of the day when sunny. Alternative spots can be found around the perimeter which provide different backgrounds and angles for photographs

Operators: Passenger scheduled services suspended
Charter and IT operators: Britannia (Boeing 767), Worldways (DC-8, TriStar), Regular freight flights by Federal Express (Boeing 747, DC-10), Air Canada (DC-8), United Parcels (DC-8), TPI International (DC-8), TNT Express (BAe 146), Air Bridge (Merchantman), USAF C-141s also stage through regularly en route Germany or Mildenhall.
The airport is used for crew training details and also by the locally-based BAe Flying Training College

Movements (1989): Total 120,451 (air transport 4,553/club 15,296/private 4,734/test and training 86,559/military 7,784). Total passengers 425,589. Over lengthy periods some very interesting movements are to be seen, but unfortunately quick visits are not always rewarded by such sights
Runways: 13/31 (9,800ft/2,987m), 03/21 (2,283ft/696m)
Radio frequencies: 118.15MHz (Tower)/120.55MHz (Approach)
Telephone: Prestwick (0292) 79822
Operated by: Prestwick Airport Ltd

Scilly Isles (St Mary's)

Although the Scilly Isles were linked to Land's End by scheduled service from 1937, it was 1940 before the present airfield was opened allowing the RAF to station a detachment of No 87 Squadron at St Mary's. Operations from the field proved very successful, Luftwaffe flying boats frequently falling victim to the squadron's Hurricanes. The civilian service to the mainland was flown throughout the war at frequencies far in excess of the prewar schedules due to the heavy demands of the military occupants. One aircraft was lost during the war, believed shot down by a patrolling Ju88.

After the war the route was maintained by BEA's Rapides, joined by several independent airlines through the years. In 1964 the fixed wing aircraft on the Land's End sector was replaced by Sikorsky S-61N helicopters, the mainland terminal moving soon afterwards to a new heliport in Penzance.

For many years the Scillies were also connected to Exeter, Bristol and Plymouth by the Twin Otters of Brymon Airways, which also gave the opportunity for onward flights to London, the Midlands, Holland and France. These benefits were lost in 1990 when the service was withdrawn. An additional link with the mainland was provided by Isles of Scilly Skybus in 1987 when it began services to Land's End/St Just using Islanders.

Despite its small size and its notorious hump-backed surface, the airfield handles a surprisingly large number of visiting light aircraft especially in the summer months. For many years any form of development was opposed, but in 1990 agreement was reached on the proposal to create a hard runway and at the same time add a modest extension to its length. Whether this will attract a new carrier remains to be seen.

Since 1983, the adjacent island of Tresco has been visited several times each day during the summer season by scheduled helicopter services from Penzance. A heliport with a 30m-square grass landing pad is provided about ¾-mile north of the southern edge of the island and is operated by Tresco estates

Location and access: Situated 1 mile east of Hugh Town on St Mary's island. A bus operated by Woodcock & Woodcock

connects with all BIH flights while a minibus service is provided by Jim Johnson for the benefit of Skybus passengers
Terminal: Contains waiting area, buffet and bar
Spectator facilities: Vicinity of terminal
Operators: Scheduled services by British International Helicopters (Sikorsky S-61N), Isles of Scilly Skybus (Islander)
Movements (1989): Total 11,792 (air transport 10,899/private 586/military 76). Total passengers 113,700
Runways: 10/28 (1,716ft/523m – grass and tarmac)
15/33 (1,870ft/570m – grass)
18/36 (1,607ft/490m – grass)
Radio frequency: 123.15MHz (Tower and Approach)
Telephone: Scillonia (0720) 22677
Operated by: Council of the Isles of Scilly

Sheffield

As long ago as 1928 the city investigated the possibility of establishing an airfield in the area, taking a positive step in 1931 by commissioning Sir Alan Cobham to inspect a site at Coal Aston to the south of Sheffield. While the report was favourable, after due consideration the council decided that no action would be taken because of the prevailing economic situation. There was then a 60-year delay before the scheme became a reality which meant that Sheffield has been the largest city in Europe without its own airport.

Fortunately the newly-formed Development Corporation began considering a project in 1988 which involved transforming a derelict site at Tinsley Park in Sheffield's Lower Don Valley. Although the area had become an industrial wasteland, the location still possessed a valuable commodity under the surface. After negotiations, agreement was finally reached in July 1989 for British Coal Opencast (BCO) to mine one million tonnes of fuel over a two-year period prior to construction of the Aerocentre. Work started on the removal of the coal in September 1989 and the task should be completed by the end of 1992.

As part of the agreement, BCO will also contribute various features for the proposed airport including the land form for the runway, access road, landscaping and drainage. This excavation and restoration work was contracted to A. F. Budge (Mining) Ltd, a member of the Retford-based A. F. Budge Construction Group. Although it is

the first time that the company has been responsible for the creation of a complete airport, it is no stranger to aviation since it operates its own airfield at nearby Gamston and has previously undertaken runway repair work for military and civil authorities.

This latest addition to the UK airport scene will possess a single runway with two access points to the apron and terminal at the western end. There will be no taxiway but this in not expected to create any problems due to the limited movements anticipated. In view of the compact size of the site, no major expansion will be possible in the future, but this is of little consequence because there is no intention to attract operators of large airliners.

The aim is to provide scheduled links with some of the larger cities such as Amsterdam, Belfast, Brussels and Paris, with Düsseldorf expected to feature at an early stage in any network of routes due to the common interests of the two industrial cities. While no direct approaches were made to any airlines, at an early stage Brymon expressed considerable interest and seems likely to be involved from the outset. A close similarity exists between its London City and Plymouth City operations so its experience could be valuable. At least Sheffield will not be limited to the Dash Seven and Dornier 228, which means that carriers employing types such as Friendships and 146s will be accepted. Unlike the Docklands airport, executive types will be permitted, although helicopters will be banned for environmental reasons. Already the BAA subsidiary, Airports UK Ltd, has been awarded the contract to operate the new airport when it becomes operational in 1993.

Location and access: Situated 3 miles northeast of the city off A630 and adjacent to the M1 at Junction 34
Terminal: Designed to handle up to 300,000 passengers per year
Spectator facilities: There should be scope for viewing around the perimeter of the site
Operators: Scheduled services will be provided by several carriers on international and domestic sectors. Types with a capacity up to 107 seats could be handled, but it is highly likely that the majority will be in the 30-seat class
Movements (1989): N/A. Total passengers initially expected to be 50,000 per year
Runway: 10/28 (3,937ft/1,200m)
Radio frequencies: N/A
Telephone: N/A
Operated by: Airports UK Ltd

Shoreham

Flying was introduced at Shoreham prior to World War I, during which various RFC squadrons were based. During the 1920s the Miles brothers were actively engaged in aircraft repair and overhaul, but it was 1934 before the airfield possessed any passenger services. Portsmouth, Southsea and Isle of Wight Aviation began by linking Shoreham with Portsmouth and Bournemouth, a route which continued to be flown until the war.

During 1939, Shoreham became the home of 16 E&RFTS, but at the outbreak of war it came into the Kenley sector as an advanced base. Numerous squadrons paid brief visits, particularly for gunnery practice in conjunction with the resident target towing Lysanders. The same type was also employed for air-sea rescue duties from the airfield. The period around D-Day saw the Spitfires of No 345 Squadron busy on operations over France, but by August 1944 the unit had moved on, the remaining occupants following suit by the end of the year.

In March 1946 the airfield was handed to the MCA, whereupon civil flying recommenced. Scheduled operations were restarted in 1948 by Brooklands Aviation using Rapides on a Shoreham-Cowes-Southampton service. The company added Jersey to their route network the following year, flown via Southampton, but at the end of the 1950 season Brooklands withdrew from the commercial scene. Other carriers were also given route approvals including Air Enterprises, Island Air Services and East Anglian Flying Services. Eventually the last named became the only airline to include Shoreham in its network, continuing until the end of 1962 when services were withdrawn.

JF Airlines introduced a new Jersey service in the early seventies, but lack of Customs at Shoreham meant that the inbound flights routed via Portsmouth. After a short break in operations, services were recommenced in the spring of 1973 to Jersey and Guernsey using an Islander and Trislander. Although successful, the airline was forced to terminate its activities with the closure of Portsmouth airport at the end of that year. Intra later acquired the licences, although the routes were flown by Haywards Aviation using an Aztec or Islander. In 1979 the company introduced a Dieppe route, while Aurigny Air Services added an Alderney to Shoreham link to its network. Neither of these carriers continued for very long on their respective sectors, although the latter was served for a time by Jersey European. The company was already flying the Jersey schedules with Twin Otters, but rationalisation in the mid-1980s found the Islanders of South East Air operating this route on the licence holder's behalf in 1986.

Prior to the following season the airline was given authority to maintain the route in its own right which resulted in the equipment being upgraded to a Twin Otter. Unfortunately this development was short-lived since the carrier was forced to cease trading in early 1988. This time there were no operators interested in taking over the Channel Islands' schedules from Shoreham, so the airport lost its limited commercial services. Nevertheless the small check-in area still displayed South-East Air's advertising in the summer of 1990 while awaiting some new enterprise to resume flights. At the beginning of the year there had been hopeful signs because Lydd-based Channel Air Shuttle submitted an application to the CAA for approval to fly on routes to Caen and Le Touquet. Hopefully this will mark a revival.

One of the airfield's major disadvantages so far as airline movements were concerned was the lack of a hard runway. This was rectified in the early 1980s by the provision of 03/21 alongside the existing grass strip. Ironically all of the services operating into Shoreham in recent years have used equipment with STOL capability, but for the future it may well be a deciding factor for airlines in doubt.

A good deal of private, club, school and executive flying takes place, added to by the activities of resident air-taxi, sales and engineering companies. Shoreham is also the HQ of the Popular Flying Association.

Location and access: Situated 1 mile west of Shoreham-by-Sea and reached from A27 or A259. Both accesses are signposted, but that via the latter passes under a bridge with 7ft headroom. Car park free. The bus service running between Brighton (Pool Valley) and Worthing passes the access road but involves a lengthy walk from the nearest stop. Journey time is about 30min
Terminal: Contains restaurant, buffet, bar and lounge area
Spectator facilities: Enclosure in front of terminal gives excellent views of movements and parked aircraft. A viewing area is also provided on the grass at the eastern perimeter. Both vantage points give good photographic opportunities, particularly when the wind is from a westerly point
Operators: Scheduled services suspended
Movements (1989): Total 66,644 (air transport 80/club 25,112/private 25,450). Total passengers 277
Runways: 03/21 (2,703ft/824m)
07/25 (2,982ft/909m – grass)
13/31 (1,394ft/425m – grass)
Radio frequencies: 125.4MHz (Tower)/123.15MHz (Approach)
Telephone: Shoreham-by-Sea (0273) 452304
Operated by: Brighton, Hove and Worthing Joint Municipal Airport Committee

Southampton (Eastleigh)

Although it was 1917 before the site was chosen by the military for development into an aircraft depot, some brief aerial excursions had been made from Eastleigh during 1910/11. With the construction of four hangars and other buildings well underway, the airfield was transferred to American control in April 1918 for use as an assembly point for equipment arriving from the US. Its active life as a Naval Air Base was short, the armistice in November almost immediately bringing a halt to any expansion. By April 1919 the Americans had gone, leaving Eastleigh to revert to RAF ownership. For a time the base was used for storage purposes, but finally it was closed in May 1920 to become the Atlantic Park Hostel, a centre for housing European immigrants awaiting transport to America.

Towards the end of the decade municipal airports were becoming popular, so it was not surprising that Southampton's civic authorities began to explore the possibilities for the city. Such sites as Fawley Marshes at Calshot and Chilworth were considered, but it was Atlantic Park which was chosen. Although purchased in 1929, it was November 1932 before Eastleigh was officially opened as an airport. Meanwhile, in the previous August, one of Sir Alan Cobham's famous air displays was held, a highlight being the arrival of Jim Mollison in his Puss Moth G-ABXY. He had used this machine when he became the first person to fly solo across the Atlantic from east to west.

A scheduled service using Airspeed Couriers was started in 1934 between Southampton and Hull, a link with Portsmouth was maintained and Railway Air Services began a mail run. With Jersey Airways moving its activities from Portsmouth in 1935, the increase in services operated was considerable. It was not long before Southampton was elevated to the ranks of the 'big four' – the others being Croydon, Heston and Liverpool. Air mail flights were introduced to the Channel Islands with the opening of the new airport at Jersey in March 1937, the inaugural sorties being in the hands of Rapide G-ADBW and DH86 G-ACYF. Impressive traffic figures were achieved with 25,266 passengers using the schedules from Southampton during the year in addition to the uplift of 700,000lb of freight and 135,000lb of mail.

Even in those days the airport enjoyed good rail and road access which accounts for its popularity. For the next couple of years or so the schedules were in the hands of Guernsey and Jersey Airways which flew to both of the main Channel Islands; Great Western and Southern Airlines with its links with Brighton and Bristol; while Portsmouth, Southsea and Isle of Wight Aviation concentrated on providing a shuttle between Southampton and Ryde, IoW. The latter was a 10min flight and was well patronised as an alternative to the sea crossing of over one hour. In 1939 the single air fare was 7/9d

(39p) with a period return set at 15/- (75p), although a day excursion was available at 1/- (5p) less.

A certain amount of traffic was lost as a result of competition from Portsmouth, Shoreham and Exeter, but plans were soon made to counter this threat. Larger airliners such as the new Flamingo were coming into service, so the authorities decided to construct a brand new, modern terminal building at an estimated cost of £50,000. Completion was expected by the end of 1939 and it was to contain full restaurant and hotel facilities. It was confidently anticipated that services to the continent would commence fairly quickly, especially since KLM had already operated a proving flight to Amsterdam and Swissair staff had inspected the airport. Understandably, however, work on the new project was shelved in view of the deteriorating European situation, but strangely it took another 50 years or so before a start on a new complex was contemplated.

Of course, the prewar operations had not been confined to civil flying with both the RAF and FAA making considerable use of the facilities. In fact the Admiralty assumed responsibility for the airfield on 1 July 1939 whereupon it was given the identity of HMS *Raven*. This nautical flavour then remained with Eastleigh until May 1946, although in the meantime scheduled air services with the Channel Islands had been resumed.

Commercial flying therefore played an important role in the life of the airport in the 1930s, but there was a significant event of 5 March 1936 that was to leave its mark on history. On this day the Spitfire was first flown after being designed and built locally.

Another company to take up residence for the production of its own aircraft was Cunliffe-Owen, although it spent much of the war modifying or assembling machines of other manufacturers. Later the twin-engined Concordia airliner was conceived, the machine first flying on 19 May 1947. Sadly there was little hope for large scale sales due to the prevailing economic situation worldwide, so production was abandoned. It also marked the end of Cunliffe-Owen's involvement in aviation, the factory becoming the property of the Ford Motor Company.

Always associated with rotary-wing designs, the Cierva Company was also installed at Eastleigh in a bid to produce its own helicopter. This was achieved, but the technique was still in its infancy and was proving expensive. After some success with the enormous Air Horse, the loss of the prototype hastened the end of an original design. Saunders-Roe took over the Eastleigh plant, remaining until it too was the subject of a take-over in 1959.

Air services began again in September 1945 when the Jersey route was reinstated, gradually increasing until by 1949 Southampton was once again amongst the busiest airports in the UK. However, without some expansion and a general improvement in the facilities on offer to both airlines and public, this position could not be maintained. Unfortunately there were no signs of any interest in the suspended 1939 project, so as an interim measure one of the original hangars was pressed into service for passenger handling. This worthy if somewhat unsuitable structure continued in this guise into the 1990s, albeit with regular improvements to its spartan interior as the years passed. Nevertheless the premises did little to revive Southampton's flagging fortunes in the immediate postwar period.

In 1952 Silver City introduced some new life by commencing a car ferry service to Cherbourg on 10 January, for which purpose two Bristol Freighters were based at the south coast airport. The carrier also proposed in 1953 to inaugurate a similar operation to Bembridge, IoW, but in the event it was not possible at the time due to bad weather delaying improvements to the island's grass airfield. Subsequently car ferry services were flown from Southampton to Jersey, Guernsey, Le Havre and Deauville with highly satisfactory results, but gradually the competition from modern ships brought an end to this enterprise.

In the meantime, on 15 June 1954 the airport became the southern terminal for the first passenger service by a British designed and built helicopter. This notable event was marked by the introduction of a link with London, the initial sortie being flown by the Bristol 171 G-AMWH which took 50min to complete the journey. Thereafter there was a return flight every weekday, but although load factors averaged 85%, it was hardly a profitable exercise, so after one year the route was suspended.

Surprisingly Southampton still had no hard runways in the late 1950s, which caused considerable problems for the heavy Freighters during wet weather. In desperation the operators were therefore obliged to move their operations to Bournemouth as a temporary measure. It could reasonably have been expected that this would have sparked a degree of interest within the Ministry of Civil Aviation, which still controlled the fortunes of the airport. Presumably the news prompted an inspection of the case because it was duly announced in 1961 that it had been decided that Southampton was no longer an economic proposition and would be closed. Fortunately, the City Corporation thought otherwise and quickly took over the airport, leasing it to Southampton Airport Ltd for operational purposes. It speeded the decision to provide a runway, the formal opening on 25 September 1965 bringing an almost immediate return of airlines from Hurn.

The destinations served changed very little for some years, the Channel Islands accounting for the majority of the schedules. As the 1980s began, so there came a marked reduction in the number of routes flown from Southampton, until in the summer of 1982 apart from Jersey and Guernsey, Air UK only connected the airport with Amsterdam, while Aurigny served Alderney. A far cry from the days of Paris, Dublin, Belfast, Brussels et al. Slowly matters began to improve, especially when the Dutch carrier NetherLines took over the Amsterdam schedules with improved frequencies in 1986. Even British Airways returned after an absence of some years, introducing an Aberdeen-Edinburgh-Birmingham-Southampton weekday return trip with HS 748s, but probably the biggest impact came in April 1987 when British Air Ferries and its subsidiary Guernsey Airlines joined Air UK on the busy sectors to the Channel Islands. Using SD3-30s, SD3-60s and Viscounts, the companies attracted a considerable amount of traffic with fares set at a reasonable level. Together the airlines gave Southampton a new lease of life, re-establishing it as a major gateway from Jersey and Guernsey.

During the summer the news was released that BAF intended to sell Guernsey Airlines to Aurigny Air Services, but it was expected that operations would continue unchanged using aircraft leased from the previous owner. It therefore came as a great blow to the airport when it was learned that the airline intended to drop Southampton completely from its schedules with effect from October. Efforts were intensified to find a new operator to restore the highly popular services, one company which submitted a licence application to the CAA being Atlantic Air Transport.

Trading as Air Atlantique, the airline was normally associated with DC-3s and cargo work, so the entry into the turbulent world of scheduled services was a new experience for the company. Certainly its approach to the operation was novel because it announced its intention to sell directly to the public rather than via the traditional travel agencies. While this was highly commendable, traditions die hard and the necessary

support was slow in materialising. Consequently after only a few weeks Air Atlantique was forced to conform and also reduce the number of daily sorties that its sole 748 G-BEKG made to Guernsey and Jersey. At the end of the summer season the services were sub-contracted to National Commuter, but following a successful application from Jersey European to take over the routes, Air Atlantique ended its association with schedules. Subsequently JEA has operated to both Jersey and Guernsey although the frequencies have not caused competing Air UK any distress.

Undoubtedly without the popular Channel Islands routes Southampton's scheduled traffic would be considerably reduced. Poor loads on the Birmingham sector were responsible for BA contracting its twice daily visit to Birmingham European in 1989, but after a year the route was suspended. On the credit side 1990 saw Capital introduce a link with Leeds using a SD3-60 until the carrier's demise, while JEA added Belfast City to its network. Internationally the airport has services to Amsterdam, Cherbourg and Paris, although the timing and frequency of the latter could be improved.

One of the more popular features of the airport for the travelling public is the close proximity of Parkway railway station. Many passengers use the economical rail-air ticket facility from London to the Channel Islands, the through journey taking about three hours.

With the demolition of the elderly decaying hangars early in 1989, the area was converted into a temporary car park with the original, more distant site relegated to serve as an overflow. It was the start of a major redevelopment project with stage one including a new terminal complex north of the existing buildings. The runway will remain unchanged since there is no wish to attract IT operators with larger types. One welcome addition will be a taxiway connecting the new apron to the northeastern end of the runway, thereby eliminating the present need to backtrack. It is hoped that the new facilities will be operational by 1992, but the construction work will not interfere with the day to day working of the airport. Relocation of the resident aviation companies will be achieved by providing accommodation on the eastern perimeter allowing the whole of the vacated site to become a business park of modern design. During the summer of 1990 the airport was sold to the BAA subsidiary, Airports UK, which had been operating it on behalf of the previous owners for some time. The development plans were unaffected by the sale.

Location and access: Situated 4 miles north-northeast of city off A355 at M27 Junction 5. Car park charges graduated. Buses pass the airport entrance on their way to and from the city, but are not particularly frequent. Trains to Parkway from Southampton Central take 7min, from Waterloo the journey time is about 80min. The station is less than 100m from the airport terminal

Terminal: The converted hangar contains a first floor bar and buffet which overlooks the apron. A very good range of snacks are available at reasonable prices. A completely new building should be in use in 1992

Spectator facilities: From the first floor buffet it is possible to observe all movements through the modern-style windows overlooking the apron. Photographs are possible with care, the glass being maintained in a much cleaner condition than in the past. Occupation of this area is not encouraged however, mainly due to its restricted size and the needs of waiting fare-paying passengers. Alternative viewing is possible at present from the long-stay car park, a vantage point which is also suitable for photographs through the 10ft-high security fence. This is more productive when the wind is from an easterly point which ensures all aircraft pass while taxying to the runway. Hopefully some thought will be given by the developers for the provision of a dedicated viewing area

Operators: Scheduled services by Air France (ATR-42, SF340), Air UK (Friendship, BAe 146), Aurigny Air Services (Trislander), Jersey European (Friendship), KLM CityHopper (Saab SF340, Fokker 50). Non-scheduled movements include the very occasional visits by transport types such as Boeing 737, Fellowship, Bandeirante and Hercules. IT programmes are usually limited to Spanish destinations but their operation very much depends upon the state of the leisure market. There is no intention to develop Southampton's participation in this field of activity.

Special events attract visitors from time to time. Light private and company operated aircraft, both UK and foreign-registered, contribute to the total movements

Movements (1989): Total 59,002 (air transport 17,927/club 20,806/private 17,588). Total passengers 493,721

Runway: 02/20 (5,653ft/1,723m)

Radio frequencies: 118.2MHz (Tower)/128.85MHz (Approach)/120.225MHz (Radar)

Telephone: Eastleigh (0703) 629600

Operated by: Airports UK Ltd

Southend (Rochford)

Flying first took place on the site in 1915, a year or so after it had been earmarked for the use of the Royal Flying Corps. For most of the war it became the home of squadrons involved in home defence, but once peace was restored Rochford was quickly returned to farmland. So it remained for over 10 years, until in 1933 Southend Corporation acquired the land in order to build an airport. Although it was September 1935 before it officially gained this status, civil flying had begun some time earlier following the creation of a local club. With the opening of the facilities, the Essex terminal of an existing ferry service to Rochester was moved to the new base, while the same year saw a Clacton-Southend-Margate operation started.

Quickly requisitioned in September 1939, all civil flying ceased and the airfield took the name of RAF Rochford for use as a satellite for Hornchurch. Various fighter squadrons spent short periods at this forward base for defence purposes before and during the Battle of Britain. In 1941 offensive fighter sweeps were mounted from Rochford, the station coming under the control of North Weald in the spring of the following year. Back with Hornchurch in 1943, Spitfires and Mustangs stayed for short periods, but already the peak activity had passed. An Armament Practice Camp was established at the airfield in February 1944, the resident Masters and Martinets dragging drogues about the sky for the benefit of the temporary visitors. With the departure of the unit Rochford spent a short time on a Care and Maintenance basis, but was reactivated as a satellite for Hornchurch in September 1944. This was to be the final change because at the end of 1945 it was closed by the Air Ministry prior to derequisitioning during the next year.

East Anglian Flying Services moved into the newly reopened airport, at first engaging in charter and pleasure flying, but by 1950 scheduled services had begun. Steadily the company grew in size, its network expanding to provide Southend with links to many destinations. Renamed Channel Airways in October 1962, the airline became the largest of those based at the airport. It therefore was a serious blow when the carrier collapsed in 1972, but fortunately other companies ensured that operations continued, albeit not on the same scale. Aviation Traders had set up an engineering facility at Southend in 1949, most of the work at first involving the maintenance of aircraft used on the Berlin Airlift. When this ended the company remained at Southend, subsequently becoming one of the largest organisations in the UK. Apart from its Carvair work, the company was responsible for the rejuvenation of the Tudors in the 1950s, a scheme to convert ex-RAF Prentices for civilian owners and the design and construction of the Accountant airliner.

In addition to IT charters by the locally-based airlines, Southend also became a busy centre of cross-Channel car ferry operations in the 1950s. Freighters were used initially, but later the locally-built Carvair took over with great success. In the face of considerable competition from the new roll-on/roll-off ships, British Air Ferries gradually ran down this type of service until by the mid-1970s they had ended. Instead the airline concentrated on passenger operations, both scheduled and charter, using Heralds. However, a further change of policy in late

1978 saw a transfer of route licences to British Island Airways, BAF reverting to purely charter and leasing activities.

After its official launch in January 1980, Air UK continued to use the Heralds leased from BAF on the services based at Southend. However, these were run down gradually both in frequency and the number of destinations on offer. In 1981 the airline formed its Air UK Commuter Services network equipped with Bandeirantes. The intention was to use the smaller aircraft on those routes with traffic of lower density. Southend qualified on this basis and although only Amsterdam, Rotterdam and Ostend were served, improvements to the timings were made to cater particularly for businessmen. Despite this effort the scheme was not particularly successful, resulting in Air UK removing its presence from Southend at the end of the 1983 summer season.

Meanwhile, a change of owner had given BAF the opportunity to expand into the scheduled market once again. Rapidly it became a busy operator, providing regular flights to the Channel Islands from an increasing number of points in the UK. In addition to possessing the largest fleet of Viscounts in the world, BAF also employed Heralds, Short SD3-30s and SD3-60s all of which used the airport for maintenance checks and overhauls at the company's engineering facility.

Unfortunately towards the end of 1987 the airline began to run into financial difficulties. Although it continued to operate freight and passenger charters, all scheduled activities were ended while a new owner was sought. Eventually the company was merged with Baltic Airlines which had been established as a Viscount operator for a short time. The restructured BAF continued to concentrate on its charter contracts with Viscounts and Heralds until in the summer of 1990 it began operating the first of two One-Elevens.

Undoubtedly Southend's scheduled traffic figures received a setback with the loss of BAF's contribution, but the airport still had a few regular services available. Maersk Air linked it with Billund in Denmark using Dash Sevens and Friendships at first, but later its new Fokker 50s were introduced on the twice-daily run. Even before the BAF cutbacks, 1987 has seen the suspension of the Rotterdam service by Holland Aero Lines. Never a particularly profitable route, the move really reflected the experiences of carriers through the years.

Fortunately there are usually newcomers willing to try again and in this case Regionair took over the Dutch sector with a Bandeirante. In the meantime locally-based National Airways had been steadily developing its charter activities, but in mid-1987 it entered the scheduled scene as National Commuter with a regular service to Brussels in conjunction with Sabena. This was followed by others to Paris and the Channel Islands while licences were obtained for various European routes, but before any further expansion was possible, the airline and its network were taken over by Regionair in late 1989. Barely six months later the latter was itself forced to cease trading due to the familiar shortage of money, but in this case a new owner was quickly found to allow a resumption of the company's activities on a reduced scale. It meant that the proposed re-equipment was shelved and the Bandeirante reinstated.

Runways had been laid in 1955, but obstructions outside the airport's boundary imposed restrictions. In order to attract the attentions of IT operators, the authorities carried out extensive ground clearance work at the threshold of Runway 06 in 1981. By removing several cottages it enabled more economic loads to be flown from the airport without the need for actual runway exten-

sion. As a result several tour companies introduced Southend to their programmes with flights to such destinations as Tenerife, Malaga and Palma. It encouraged further improvements, this time with the reconstruction and modernisation of the terminal in 1986. General improvements to the runway and taxiways were completed during the next couple of years or so, in order to attract even more IT traffic.

Despite this effort there was no dramatic increase in the degree of interest displayed. Southend-based Burstin Travel had endured much inconvenience due to the unreliability and general indifference of its contracted carriers, so it decided to launch its own airline to overcome this handicap which hitherto had given a poor impression to its clients. Accordingly in the spring of 1990 Princess Air began an impressive programme of IT flights, both from its home base and other UK airports. A BAe 146-200QC had been chosen so that a high rate of utilisation could be maintained by using the machine for night cargo work.

There is considerable scope for this type of business to be developed at the Essex airport, but the local council limits the number of night freight flights to 182 per week – a surprising restriction considering it is the owner of the site. Presumably it depends on whether income or votes are more important. Nevertheless there is a wide selection of destinations flown by a number of different aircraft, but with little prospect of significant growth in the near future. Use of larger, quieter types such as the 146 would certainly improve matters.

The anti-airport lobby received more encouragement at the end of 1990 when Maersk moved its operation to Gatwick, the Billund sector passing to Sun-Air. Shortly after this blow, Southend lost Regionair when the company ended its scheduled flying in January 1991, followed two months later by the demise of Princess Air, the victim of the prevailing economic gloom.

Location and access: Situated 2 miles north of Southend, off the A127. Car park charges graduated. Southend Corporation minibus route 65 serves the airport from the Central bus station with a journey time of about 10min
Terminal: Contains lounge area with buffet which produces hot snacks in addition to sandwiches and cakes. The windows in the

bar overlook the apron and provide reasonable views. The first floor restaurant offers similar facilities. There is also a shop in the terminal which offers a good range of aviation books and magazines

Spectator facilities: A small fenced area has been provided between the terminal and control tower which offers good views and the possibility of photographs.

Due to the close proximity of the subjects, it is necessary to ensure that the lens is not including the mesh of the 10ft-security fence in its coverage.Further along similar vantage points exist in the car park adjacent to the light aircraft area. Photographs can also be obtained from this point. Good landing shots can be taken at the threshold of runway 06 in Eastwoodbury Lane when the wind is from the northeast

Operators: Scheduled services by Sun-Air

(Citation), British Air Ferries (Viscount - freight)

Charter and IT carriers: BAF (Viscount, Herald, One-Eleven), Air Malta (Boeing 737). Other freight carriers include BAC Charters (Twin Otter, Bandeirante) and Channel Express.

A considerable number of movements are made by club, private and company aircraft, both UK and foreign registered, when using the airport as a gateway into and out of the country

Movements (1989): Total 91,920 (air transport 10,383/club 52,952/private 18,293). Total passengers 99,499

Runway: 06/24 (5,265ft/1,605m)

Radio frequencies: 127.725MHz (Tower)/128.95MHz (Approach)

Telephone: Southend (0702) 340201

Operated by: Airports UK Ltd

Stansted

The airfield was built for and by the US forces in World War 2, work starting in August 1942. Known as Station 169, from August 1943 the base became responsible for the handling of damaged aircraft and maintaining the supply of replacements to operational groups. On 9 February 1944 the 344th Bomb Group moved in equipped with B-26 Marauders. Many of the operations flown from Stansted were in support of the

invasion of France and the subsequent advances. The Group transferred to a continental base in September 1944, leaving the airfield to return to its role of a Tactical Air Depot.

After the war the RAF took over, setting up 263 MU on the base, whose task it was to dispose of the vast quantities of surplus stores. By December 1946 it was possible for a civilian operator to join the dwindling RAF personnel, the Halifax sorties of London Aero and Motor Services launching

Stansted as a cargo centre. Despite the initial success, LAMS was wound up in July 1948, leaving the smaller but active Kearsley Airways to maintain charters with Dakotas from the airfield, until it too ceased commercial flying two years later. In this case it was a voluntary decision, the company preferring to continue in an engineering role as they have to the present day. The Ministry of Civil Aviation assumed control of Stansted in 1949, moving their flying unit from Gatwick soon afterwards. It has remained ever since.

In the 1950s several carriers flew long distance charters especially on Government contracts, while considerable airfield development was undertaken by the Americans with a view to using it as a strategic base. The resultant 10,000ft runway certainly enhanced its future as an airport.

The 1960s found Stansted developing once again as a major freight centre with both Lloyd International and Transmeridian building up their businesses with Britannias and CL-44s. This activity continued until the collapse of British Cargo Airlines in March 1980 drastically reduced the amount of freight handled. It came at an unfortunate time since a brand new cargo terminal had just been completed. Gradually however this type of traffic has picked up due to the locally based HeavyLift and Instone Air Line plus overseas carriers using Stansted on a regular basis.

Passenger traffic increased enormously with the arrival of Channel Airways who operated both schedules and ITs with Viscounts, One-Elevens, Tridents and Comets. In February 1972 once again Stansted witnessed the departure of its major residents when Channel ceased operations, followed soon afterwards by Lloyd.

During Channel's occupation, a brand new terminal had been built, replacing the buildings built for the 344th Bomb Group a quarter of a century earlier. The improvements attracted several foreign airlines engaged in charter work, but after a time the US carriers began to favour Gatwick. European companies continued to support the airport in varying degrees, the Scandinavian airlines proving the most consistent.

After the demise of Channel, scheduled services were restricted to a single seasonal Jersey flight by British Midland until 1 November 1978. Air Anglia then introduced a weekday service to Norwich and the north, which was greatly expanded in the summer of the following year.

A nominal change of carrier took place in January 1980 when Air UK was launched. The new airline continued the reduced winter timings on the Norwich route, a trend also noted during the following summer. The company found it necessary to suspend its Stansted operations completely at the end of 1980, eventually to return to introduce an Amsterdam link in November 1981. With slight adjustments, this service has continued to be included in the Air UK programme. Two other international licences were won in the early 1980s, namely Brussels and Paris. It was intended that initially they would form a Bandeirante network, the latter sector pending French approval. It was some time before either route was introduced; in fact the airline lost the Brussels licence to Jersey European, the company starting services in the spring of 1982.

This carrier had first served Stansted in 1980, when a schedule to the Channel Islands was launched. The frequencies offered were a marked improvement on those available for some years, although by 1982 the size of equipment had shrunk from Viscount/Herald to Bandeirante and later Twin Otter operations. Both of the latter types were also employed on the link between Stansted, Liverpool and Dublin, services which were inaugurated in December 1981. Poor results quickly brought an end to this route, a fate also suffered by that to the Belgian capital. Air UK applied to the CAA to take over the Brussels licence, this time starting up shortly after authority was received. Flown at first by Bandeirantes, increasing traffic soon justified larger aircraft. Further international routes have subsequently been added while approval has been received for several others. Competition came in April 1987 when Air France began a twice-daily schedule to Paris using Saab 340As, but the timings did not affect the British company unduly. Similarly KLM joined it on the popular Amsterdam sector, although this time it was under a pool arrangement. However, by the start of the 1988 summer season the Dutch carrier realised it was more sensible for Air UK to resume responsibility for all Schiphol flights. Domestic services were not overlooked by Air UK as requests were made in 1987 for both Belfast and Glasgow to be added to the network so that the Stansted hub could be built up in readiness for the completion of London's third airport. Additionally the company, together with British & Commonwealth

Holdings and the Viking International Group, announced the creation of a new carrier in June 1987 to operate ITs from its Stansted base. Known as Air UK (Leisure) Ltd, arrangements were made so that two leased Boeing 737-200s could begin flying for the airline in April 1988. In October the first 737-400 was delivered, the type chosen for the permanent fleet which was due to be six-strong by spring 1991.

With Stansted's future secure at last, several new carriers were attracted to the airport, one such company being Highland Express. Equipped with a single Boeing 747, after much time in the planning stage the airline finally began operations at the beginning of June 1987, staging through Prestwick en route to New York several times per week. This venture was relatively short-lived, ending in December with the collapse of the carrier. London Express was another that hoped to begin commercial flying with a 747, the destinations proposed for its regular sorties all being in the Far East. Financial problems postponed the launch planned for the autumn of 1986, but the company was still confident that it would be able to start up some time in the future. Indeed in early 1988 preparations were underway for operations to begin in the summer by Swan Airlines, the successor to London Express. This also failed to materialise.

Thurston Aviation moved its activities to Stansted in 1978, at the same time offering a handling service for the operators of executive aircraft. The company later set up Tal-Air, a carrier which then became involved in the movement of small packets and parcels to the Brussels hub of Federal Express. This American freight airline began flying to Europe in 1985 employing specially modified Boeing 727s for the lengthy run from Memphis. It was not long before DC-10-30s were substituted, the type staging through the Essex airport on four days each week while en route to Brussels. A rejuvenated Tradewinds moved its operating base from Gatwick to join HeavyLift Cargo Airlines at Stansted in 1986, but on the debit side Instone moved out to Coventry.

Aviation Traders (ATEL) was established at the airport for many years, undertaking maintenance overhauls and conversions on a wide range of types particularly Boeing 707s. Some years ago the company became a subsidiary of Aer Lingus, but in March 1987 ATEL was acquired by the privately-owned Qualitair Group of Cambridge.

In conjunction with the airport's expansion, the new owner built an engineering facility at the airport which was sufficiently large to enable it to take two Boeing 747s or up to 10 Boeing 737s. In September 1989 the company was acquired by the Swedish group, FFV Aerotech.

Stansted's future as London's third airport was the subject of many debates and inquiries, but the uncertainty ended when work finally started on its development in April 1986. Access roads and car parks were laid at remarkable speed, while the site for the proposed terminal was enthusiastically attacked by scrapers and similar earth-moving devices. Long-standing landmarks disappeared to make way for the new structures which began to take shape at an early stage. Meanwhile the contractors were busy with the rail spur from the main line just north of Stansted station. This involved a tunnel under the airport but the work was completed in 1989 in readiness for track laying and the erection of the overhead wires. When completed, BR trains equipped with new rolling stock will link the airport with London (Liverpool Street) at half-hourly intervals. The terminal has been designed to present a spacious appearance with all passenger activity at one floor level. Most travellers will be transported to and from the aircraft via a tracked transit link to a satellite building containing the departure lounge and airbridges. A second unit will open in 1993 as the demand exceeds the annual 8 million capacity designed for the March 1991 opening.

Location and access: Situated off the A120 three miles from Bishop's Stortford with direct access from M11 Junction 8. Both short and long-term car parks are available with charges graduated to NCP standards. Regular trains run to and from Liverpool Street at 30min intervals with a journey time of 40min. A service also operates to Cambridge and the north. Eastern National bus routes 33, 123, 233, 333, 305, 370 and X70 operate to neighbouring towns while Cambridge Coach Services and National Express include the airport in their networks. There is a service that links Stansted with Heathrow, Gatwick and Cambridge

Terminal: Ramps, escalators and lifts give passengers direct access from the BR station, car park and coach stands to the

single floor allocated for the usual processing arrangements. It also contains refreshment facilities, shop and bank
Spectator facilities: As the developed airport took shape in the late 1980s, so the useful vantage points around the perimeter steadily disappeared. By mid-1990 it was virtually impossible to acquire any ground shots due to the erection of fences, buildings and other obstructions. This left landing shots as the only option depending upon wind direction and time of day. Even these may be affected in the future due to the planting of 250,000 trees around the site. It has been stated by the BAA that it is intended to provide a spectators' enclosure near to the terminal. At least it will probably meet the requirements for viewing, but is unlikely to be particularly useful for photography due to its position behind the transit link, service roads and at least two security fences
Operators: Scheduled services by Air France (ATR42, Saab SF340, Fellowship), Air UK (Friendship, BAe 146), KLM CityHopper (Saab SF340, Fokker 50), Jersey European (Friendship), Noble Air (Boeing 727), Ryanair (One-Eleven, ATR-42), TAT (Friendship), Crossair (BAe 146), Company scheduled flights by Ford Motor Co (One-Eleven, Gulfstream 1).
Regular cargo flights by HeavyLift Cargo Airlines (Belfast, Conroy CL-44, CL-44J), Federal Express (DC-10), Iberia (Boeing 727), Sabena (Boeing 737), British Air Ferries (Friendship), United Parcels (DC-8) and Aeroflot (IL-76). Mail and newspaper

flights by BAC Charter (Twin Otter, Bandeirante)
Charter and IT operators: Aeroflot (Tu-134), Airtours (MD-83), Air Atlantis (Boeing 737), Air Liberte (MD-83), Air Malta (Boeing 737), Air Transat (TriStar), American Trans Air (TriStar, Boeing 757), Air UK Leisure (Boeing 737), Adria (DC-9, Airbus A320), African Safari (DC-8), Aviogenex (Boeing 737), Balkan (Tu-154), Braathens (Boeing 737), Britannia Airways (Boeing 737), British Air Ferries (One-Eleven), Busy Bee (Friendship, Boeing 737), Conair (Airbus A300), Dan-Air (Boeing 727, One-Eleven), Futura (Boeing 737), JAT (DC-9), Monarch (Boeing 757), Nationair (Boeing 757), Noble Air (Boeing 727), Scanair/SAS (DC-9/10, MD-80), Spanair (MD-80), Sterling (Boeing 727/757, Caravelle), Titan Airways (Bandeirante, Short SD3-30), Transwede (MD-80, Caravelle, Boeing 737), Worldways (DC-8, TriStar). Stansted often takes diversions from fog or strike-bound Heathrow, Gatwick, Luton or Norwich. Crew training is also carried out by airlines and flying schools
Movements (1989): Total 51,420 (air transport 26,226/club 1,054/private 9,565/test and training 6,855/empty 6,754). Total passengers 1,375,311
Runway: 05/23 (10,000ft/3,048m)
Radio frequencies: 118.15MHz (Tower)/125.55MHz, 126.95MHz (Approach)
Telephone: Bishop's Stortford (0279) 502380
Operated by: Stansted Airport Ltd

Teesside (Middleton St George)

The airport's early days followed a familiar pattern since it was built as an RAF station. Taking the name of Middleton St George, its first resident was the Whitley V-equipped No 78 Squadron which arrived on 10 April 1941, staying some seven months. It returned for a further short spell in 1942, this time using Halifax IIIs. It meant that Middleton now had two Halifax units as No 76 Squadron had been at the base since June 1941. During the course of its many operations, it had in fact become the first unit to drop the 8,000lb bomb, an event which occurred on 10/11 April 1942 during a raid on Essen.

By October 1942, both founder members had departed, the vacant airfield quickly

receiving Nos 419 and 420 Squadrons, RCAF, the latter being replaced by another Canadian squadron, No 428, in June 1943. The two units remained at Middleton until the end of the war, exchanging their Halifaxes for Lancaster Xs for the last year of operational service in the UK.

After the war, the airfield was earmarked for development as a fighter base. However, it was used as a training establishment for some years, housing 13 OTU, 2 ANS and 205 AFS at various times. Operational life began again in February 1957 when Nos 92 and 264 Squadrons arrived using Hunter F6s and Meteor NF14s respectively. Middleton was without aircraft for a period in 1957/58 to allow a considerable modernisation programme to be completed. The Hunters of No 92 Squadron returned, but in the meantime No 264 had exchanged the Meteors for the later Javelin and had become No 33 Squadron, subsequently remaining at Middleton until its eventual disbandment in November 1962. Its companion No 92 Squadron, became Fighter Command's official aerobatic team known as the Blue Diamonds, leaving the base in May 1961.

The supersonic age arrived in June 1962 when the Lightning Conversion Squadron was formed with the first two-seater Mk 4s. It was renamed 226 OCU on 1 June 1963, soon afterwards adding some Mk 1s to its inventory. In October of that year it was announced that the RAF was vacating the airfield, mainly on grounds of economy. The OCU moved out on 13 April 1964 with Middleton passing to the local authorities for the sum of £340,000.

Now known as Teesside, civil flying commenced on 1 October with the first scheduled service two weeks later to Manchester. BKS soon added others including routes to Amsterdam, Belfast, Dublin, Düsseldorf and London.

Towards the end of 1966 BKS withdrew its operations, Autair acquiring the London licence. The airline used Heralds on the route with Luton as the southern terminus, which was later changed to Heathrow. Teesside became one of the halts for the imaginative bus-stop service started by Channel Airways in January 1969. It was

then possible to travel northwards to Aberdeen via Newcastle and Edinburgh, or south to Stansted via Leeds and East Midlands with connections available to other airports such as Southend and Norwich. It unfortunately lasted only ten months, the airport losing a very useful facility.

At this time Autair dropped out of the scheduled scene, the London service being taken over by British Midland who have held the licence to the present day. Air Anglia began its use of the airport in 1972, adding it as an intermediate stop on the Norwich-Aberdeen route, a service continued by its successor, Air UK. The new airline soon began to prune its network however, one of the casualties being the Glasgow link which was transferred to the locally based Casair Aviation. This company continued to operate it with Navajos, expanding its Teesside network in 1982 to include Gatwick and Belfast on weekdays. For this purpose a Short SD3-30 was acquired, further employment being found for it when a couple of seasonal weekend services were introduced to Guernsey and the Isle of Man. In the autumn of 1982 the carrier merged with Eastern and Genair, operations continuing under the latter name until its demise in 1984. Casair subsequently resumed flying under its original title, taking over the Glasgow and Humberside sectors from the licence holder, Air Ecosse, but in March 1988 the company once again ceased its activities.

Dan-Air has maintained a token presence although its contribution is restricted to a transit stop each weekday by a BAe 146 linking Newcastle with Amsterdam and a few IT flights. In recent years there has been little change in the scheduled scene although Air Kilroe's Jetstream now shuttles between the airport and Manchester five times each weekday on behalf of ICI. Similarly there has been little growth in leisure traffic with a few new destinations on offer to the local catchment area.

Location and access: Situated on the A67, 6 miles east of Darlington. Direction signs can easily be followed from the A1(M) and A66(M) to airport. Car park has graduated charges. United bus service from Darlington Feethams runs every 30min taking 25min for the journey. Trains from Middlesbrough stop at the airport station every 30min with a journey time of 20min. From Stockton the service is hourly, journey time being 20min. A coach connects the station with the airport terminal

Terminal: Comprises modern single-storey buildings, containing a buffet, restaurant, bar, shop and lounge area, while the original officers' mess nearby has been converted into the well equipped St George Hotel

Spectator facilities: A roof terrace is provided from where viewing is generally satisfactory. As a photographic vantage point it poses problems due to it being set back from the front of the building. In any event on bright days conditions are more favourable in the afternoons

Operators: Scheduled services by Air Kilroe (Jetstream), Air UK (Friendship), British Midland (DC-9), Dan-Air (BAe 146) *Charter and IT operators:* Adria Airways (DC-9), Aviogenex (Boeing 737), British Midland (DC-9), Dan-Air (BAe 146, Boeing 727/737), JAT (DC-9), Oasis (MD-80)

Air-Taxi and other light aircraft including those of the Cleveland Flying School are based at Teesside

Movements (1989): Total 63,095 (air transport 9,718/club 43,312/private 4,295/test and training 2,755). Total passengers 361,595

Runways: 05/23 (7,516ft/2,291m) 01/19 (2,428ft/740m)

Radio frequencies: 119.8MHz (Tower)/118.85MHz (Approach)/ 128.85MHz (Radar)

Telephone: Darlington (0325) 332811

Operated by: Teesside International Airport Ltd

Wick

Wick was opened as a grass airfield in 1935, receiving the scheduled services of Aberdeen Airways and Highland Airways. Operations continued until 1939 although the latter company had by this time become a part of Scottish Airways. At the outbreak of war the airfield was taken over by the Air Ministry, becoming an important base for both Fighter and Coastal Command squadrons operating over the North Sea and Scandinavia. It also saw BOAC Mosquitos engaged on the Swedish diplomatic service when they called for refuelling.

Airline services were expanded after the war, this time from a much larger and better equipped airfield. Both Scottish and Allied Airways served Wick in the immediate postwar period, but the operations were soon taken over by BEA.

The routes never proved a very profitable part of the airline's network, especially when eventually it was necessary to employ Viscounts on the services. British Airways began to withdraw some of the short stage Highland and Island routes including some from Wick in 1976. Loganair took over the responsibility for these links, initially using Islanders and Trislanders, although the latter type was replaced by Twin Otters after a time.

Until the early 1980s, British Airways continued to ply a couple of routes to Aberdeen and the Shetlands using BAe 748s and Viscounts, but eventually the airline pulled out of Wick. The airport gained the services of Air Ecosse, a comparative newcomer to the scheduled scene. It took over the Aberdeen licence, also adding Sumburgh and the Faroe Islands to its expanding network using Twin Otters and Bandeirantes. Varying fortunes created the need for several reorganisations within this airline, until finally in early 1987 financial problems forced it to suspend operations. Peregrine had been operating some of the services for Air Ecosse, but at this point there was a general scramble for the licences held by the latter. Leading these applications was British Airways which wanted to win back the Aberdeen-Wick route, a wish granted by the

CAA. Strong protests were made by Air Ecosse at the loss of what was one of the company's most lucrative sectors. It was especially important because attempts were being made to attract a new owner, but despite several approaches it was not until late 1988 that the carrier was taken over by Peregrine. By 1990 BA had found that Wick still did not generate a great deal of traffic on the Edinburgh sector, so in the absence of a small-capacity type, the airline subcontracted the operation so that Bandeirantes and Gulfstream 1s were introduced to the twice-daily, Mondays to Fridays, schedules. As an alternative the local population can choose to fly to Edinburgh or Kirkwall with Loganair.

Occasional visits are made by executive and light aircraft in connection with North Sea oil work or the nearby atomic power plant at Dounreay.

Location and access: Signposted off A9 in town of Wick. Situated on outskirts. Car park free
Terminal: Small single-storey building containing lounge. Buffet facility
Spectator facilities: Good viewng from vicinity of terminal. Photographic opportunities good using a standard or telephoto lens
Operators: Scheduled services by Loganair (Short SD3-60, Islander), British Airways (Bandeirante, Gulfstream 1 – subcontracted)
Movements (1989): 5,667 (air transport 5,008/club 202/empty positioning 117/private 146). Total passengers 47,989
Runways: 08/26 (3,399ft/1,036m), 14/32 (5,279ft/1,609m)
Radio frequency: 119.7MHz (Tower)
Telephone: Wick (0955) 2215
Operated by: Highlands and Islands Airports Ltd

Airfields guide

In this section brief notes are given of location and use of airfields not covered earlier, including those serving the northern islands and Alderney with scheduled operations. Excluded are the vast majority of private airstrips.

Aberporth (Dyfed) North side of A487, 5 miles northeast of Cardigan. RAE. Communications aircraft

Abingdon (Oxon) West of A34 and B4017, 5 miles south-southwest of Oxford. RAF MU for Jaguars, Hunters and Hawks. Oxford & London UAS Bulldogs

Alconbury (Cambs) Near junction of A14 and A1, 4 miles northwest of Huntingdon. USAF 10 TFW A-10s, 17 RW TR-1s

Alderney (Channel Isle) Southwest of island, 1 mile from St Anne. Civil. Aurigny services to south coast and France. TWR 125.35MHz

Andover (Hants) West of town south of A303. AAC helicopters. Middle Wallop satellite

Andrewsfield (Essex) Between Gt Dunmow and Braintree to north of A120 towards Saling and Stebbing. Civil. Light aircraft. A/G 130. 55MHz

Audley End (Essex) One mile west of Saffron Walden off A130. Civil. Light aircraft. A/G 122.35MHz

Badminton (Avon) Six miles east-northeast of Chipping Sodbury off B4040. Civil. Light aircraft. A/G 123.175MHz

Barra (Western Isles) On foreshore of Traigh Mhor. Civil. Loganair services, air taxi operations. A/G 130.65MHz

Barrow/Walney Island (Cumbria) Two miles northwest of town at north end of island. Civil. Operated by Vickers Ltd. Executive aircraft. TWR 123.2MHz

Barton (Greater Manchester) Five miles west of Manchester to north side of A57 and 1 mile west of M62 Junction 2. Civil. Light aircraft. A/G 122.7MHz

Battersea (London) South bank of Thames west of Battersea Bridge. Westland Heliport. Civil and military helicopters. TWR 122.9MHz

Beccles (Suffolk) Two miles southeast of town north side of B1127. Civil. British International Helicopters. A/G 134.6MHz

Benbecula (Western Isles) Northwest side of island north of B892. Civil. Loganair, British Airways services. TWR 119.2MHz

Benson (Oxon) Ten miles southeast of Oxford 1 mile northeast of Wallingford by A423. RAF, Queen's Flight aircraft. No 115 Sqn Andovers

Bentwaters (Suffolk) Southeast of B1069. Six miles northeast of Woodbridge village. USAF 81TFW A-10s

Bicester (Oxon) Two miles northeast of town east side of A421. RAF Gliding and Soaring Association. Light aircraft

Biggin Hill (Kent) East side of A233, 4 miles north of Westerham. Civil. Light and executive aircraft. Warbirds of GB base. APP 129.4MHz. TWR 134.8MHz

Binbrook (Lincs) Ten miles southwest of Grimsby north of B1203. RAF

Birkdale Sands (Merseyside) South of Southport west of A565. Civil seasonal pleasure flying with light aircraft and helicopters

Blackbushe (Hants) Four miles west of Camberley, north side of A30. Civil. Light and company aircraft. A/G 122.3MHz

Bodmin (Cornwall) To south of A30(T), 2 miles NE of Bodmin. Civil. Light aircraft. A/G 122.7MHz

Booker/Wycombe Air Park (Bucks) Three miles southwest of High Wycombe east of B482. Civil. Light aircraft. Personal Plane Services. A/G 126.55MHz

Boscombe Down (Wilts) Five miles north of Salisbury east of A345, south of A303 at Amesbury. MOD, A & AEE. Empire Test Pilots School. Test and research aircraft

Bourn (Cambs) Seven miles west of Cambridge south side of A45. Civil. Light aircraft, helicopters, crop sprayers. A/G 129.8MHz

Brawdy (Dyfed) Nine miles northwest of Haverfordwest north of A487. RAF No 1 TWU (Nos 79 & 234 Sqns) Hawks, No 202 Sqn B Flt SAR helicopters

Brize Norton (Oxon) Five miles southwest of Witney west of A4095, east of B4020. RAF No 10 Sqn VC-10s, No 101 Sqn VC10 tankers, No 216 Sqn TriStar

Brough (Humberside) Six miles west of Hull, 2 miles south of A63. British Aerospace works. TWR 130.55MHz. APP 118.225MHz

Catterick (Yorks) East of A1 south of town. RAF. Firefighting training school, 645 VGS Grob Viking

Chalgrove (Oxon) Eight miles southeast of Oxford on north side of B480. Civil. Martin Baker Ltd

Challock (Kent) Three miles west of village south of A252. Civil. Light aircraft. Kent Gliding Club

Chester (Cheshire) See Hawarden

Chetwynd (Shropshire) Three miles north of Newport east of A41. RAF. RLG for Shawbury

Chirk (Clwyd) East of A5, 1 mile north of village, 5 miles east of Llangollen. Civil. Light aircraft. Restorations

Chivenor (Devon) Four miles west of Barnstaple south of A361. RAF. No 22 Sqn A Flt SAR Helicopters, No 2 TWU (Nos 63 & 151 Sqns) Hawks

Church Fenton (Yorks) Six miles northwest of Selby southwest of B1223, north of B1222. RAF RLG for Linton. No 7 FTS Jet Provosts, Tucanos, gliders. TWR/APP 126.5MHz

Clacton (Essex) West of town near holiday camp. Civil seasonal pleasure flying A/G 122.325MHz

Colonsay (Strathclyde Reg) West end of island. Civil. Loganair flights

Coltishall (Norfolk) Nine miles north of Norwich to west of B1150. RAF Nos 6, 41 and 54 Sqns Jaguars. No 22 Sqn A Flt. SAR helicopters

Compton Abbas (Dorset) East of minor road to Blandford Forum, 2 miles south of B3081, 2 miles east of Shaftesbury. 800ft hill involved. Civil. Light aircraft. A/G 122.7MHz

Coningsby (Lincs) One mile south of A153, west of B1192, 15 miles northeast of Sleaford. RAF Nos 29 Sqn and 229 OCU Tornado (No 65 Sqn)

Cosford (Shropshire) Nine miles northwest of Wolverhampton west of A41 northwest of Albrighton. RAF Technical Training. Birmingham UAS Bulldogs. Aerospace museum

Cottesmore (Leics) Four miles northeast of Oakham, north of B668. RAF. TTTE Tornado base

Cranfield (Beds) Four miles east of M1 between Junctions 13 and 14. North of A5140. Civil. Institute of Technology. Cessna agent. TWR 123.2MHz. APP 122.85MHz

Cranwell (Lincs) Four miles northwest of Sleaford to north of A17 and astride B1429. RAF College No 3 FTS. Jet Provosts, Tucano

Crosland Moor (Yorks) Three miles southwest of Huddersfield off A62. Civil. Light aircraft. A/G 122.2MHz

Crowland (Lincs) Six miles south of Spalding off A1073. Civil. Light aircraft

Culdrose (Cornwall) One mile southeast of Helston east of A3083. RN helicopters, Jetstreams. TWR 122.1MHz, APP 134.05MHz

Cumbernauld (Strathclyde Reg) Six miles west-southwest of Falkirk, north of A80. Civil. Light aircraft TWR 120.6MHz

Denham (Bucks) From A40 west of A412, 1 mile north of A40 and M40 Junction 1. Civil. Light aircraft. A/G 130.725MHz

Dishforth (Yorks) Four miles east of Ripon, east side of A1. RAF. RLG for Linton. Gliders TWR 122.1MHz, APP 129.15MHz

Doncaster (Yorks) One mile southeast of town south of A638 opposite racecourse. Civil. Light aircraft. A/G 122.9MHz

Dornoch (Highland Reg) South of town on A949, east of A9. Civil. Light aircraft

Dounreay (Highland Reg) Eight miles west of Thurso north of A836. Civil. Executive and light aircraft. Serves atomic power station. TWR/APP 122.4MHz

Dunkeswell (Devon) Five miles northwest of Honiton west of minor road A30 to Hemyock. Civil. Light aircraft. A/G 123.475MHz

Dunsfold (Surrey) Nine miles south of Guildford, west of A281, south of B2130, east of village. British Aerospace plant. Harriers, Hawks, Hunters

Duxford (Cambs) Nine miles south of Cambridge, eight miles east of Royston south side of A505. M11 Junction 10 adjacent. Civil. Historic Aviation Centre. IWM, Duxford Aviation Society etc. A/G 123.5MHz

Earls Colne (Essex) Five miles southeast of Halstead off A604. Civil. Light aircraft. A/G 122.425MHz

East Fortune (Lothian) South of B1377, 3 miles north of East Linton and A1. Civil. Light aircraft. Museum of Flight

Eday (Orkney) West of B9063 centre of island. Civil. Loganair services

Eglinton (N. Ireland) Seven miles north of Londonderry on A2. Civil. Light aircraft Loganair schedules with SD3-60s

Elstree (Herts) West from A5183 on to A411 in village for short distance before right on minor road. Civil. Light and executive aircraft. A/G 122.4MHz

Enniskillen (N. Ireland) Five miles north of town off A32. Civil. Light aircraft. A/G 123.2MHz

Enstone (Oxon) Five miles southeast of Chipping Norton north of A34, east of B4022, 1 mile from village. Civil. Light aircraft

Fairford (Glos) North of Swindon, 4 miles west of Lechlade south of A417. USAF

Fair Isle (Shetland Isles) Centre of island. Civil. Loganair services

Fairoaks (Surrey) Three miles north of

Woking to south of A319. Civil. Executive and light aircraft. A/G 123.425MHz

Farnborough (Hants) West of A325 north of A323. MOD. RAE research aircraft

Fearn (Highland Reg) Ten miles northeast of Invergordon (Cromarty Firth) south of B9166. Civil. Light aircraft

Felthorpe (Norfolk) Eight miles northwest of Norwich, south of village, west of minor road, north of A1067, 2 miles east of Attlebridge. Civil. Light aircraft. A/G 123.5MHz

Fenland (Lincs) South of minor road, 1 mile west of B1168, 5 miles south of A151 at Holbeach. Civil. Light aircraft. A/G 122.925MHz

Fetlar (Shetland) Centre of island. Civil. Loganair services

Filton/Bristol (Avon) Four miles north of city west of A38. British Aerospace. Test airfield. VC-10 conversion, Bristol UAS Bulldogs, Rolls-Royce aircraft. Airbus components, USAF F-111 overhauls. No 3 AEF Chipmunks. TWR 124.95MHz, APP 122.725MHz

Finmere (Bucks) Three miles west of Buckingham south of A421 (near junction with B4031). Civil. Light aircraft

Finningley (Yorks) Between A638 and A614 north of Bawtry and south of B1396, southeast of Doncaster. RAF No 6 FTS. Dominies, Jet Provosts, Jetstreams, York UAS Bulldogs, No 9 AEF Chipmunks

Flotta (Orkney) Centre of island west of B9045. Civil. Oil charter traffic. A/G 122.15MHz

Fordoun (Grampian Reg) South of B966, 1 mile west of A94, 9 miles southwest of Stonehaven. Civil. Light aircraft

Gamston (Notts) West of B6387, north of A1, 3 miles south of Retford. Civil. Light aircraft. A/G 130.475MHz

Glenrothes (Fife Reg) Two miles southwest of town, east of B922, north of B921, west of A94. A/G 130.45MHz

Goodwood (Sussex) Off A285 north of Chichester. Civil. Light aircraft. TWR 120.65MHz, APP 122.45MHz

Gt Yarmouth/North Denes (Norfolk) On west side of A149, 2 miles north of Gt Yarmouth. Civil. Light aircraft. Pleasure flying. North Sea oil helicopter traffic. A/G 120.45MHz

Greenham Common (Berks) North of A339, 2 miles east of A34, southeast of Newbury. USAF reserve base

Halfpenny Green (Staffs) Five miles east of Bridgnorth, southwest of Wolverhampton

off B4176. Civil. Light aircraft. A/G 123.0MHz

Halton (Bucks) Three miles southeast of Aylesbury, north of A4011, south of B4544. RAF Technical Training

Hatfield (Herts) West side of A1(M) 3 miles northeast of St Albans. British Aerospace factory. BAe 146 production. TWR 130.8MHz, APP 123.35MHz

Haverfordwest (Dyfed) East of A40, 2 miles north of town. Civil. Light and executive aircraft. A/G 122.2MHz

Hawarden (Cheshire) Four miles west-southwest of Chester north of A55. British Aerospace 125s. TWR 124.95MHz, APP 123.35MHz

Headcorn (Kent) Southeast of village east of A274 about 9 miles southeast of Maidstone. Civil. Light aircraft. Crop sprayers. Lashenden Air Warfare Museum. Parachute School. A/G 122.0MHz

Henlow (Beds) East side of A600 at junction with A6001, 2 miles southeast of Shefford. RAF. Museum store

Henstridge (Somerset) South of A30, 2 miles east of A357. Civil. Light aircraft

Hethel (Norfolk) Near East Carleton between A11 and B1113, 7 miles southwest of Norwich. Civil. Light aircraft. Lotus cars. A/G 122.35MHz

Holme-on-Spalding Moor (Humberside) On east side of A614, northeast of Goole and Howden. British Aerospace. TWR 130.55MHz, APP 122.55MHz

Honington (Suffolk) North of Bury St Edmunds between A143 and A1088, 5 miles south of Thetford. RAF TWCU (No 45 Sqn) and No 13 Sqn Tornados

Hoy/Longhope (Orkney) Half mile southwest of Longhope. Civil. Loganair services

Hucknall (Notts) One mile southwest of Hucknall, south of B6009. Civil. Rolls-Royce. Light aircraft. A/G 130.8MHz

Islay/Port Ellen (Strathclyde Reg) South end of island west of A846. Civil. Loganair services. TWR/APP 123.15MHz

Kemble (Glos) Northwest of A429, south of A433, 4 miles southwest of Cirencester. RAF. TWR/APP 118.9MHz

Kidlington (Oxon) Six miles northwest of Oxford north side of connecting road between A34 and A423 from village. Civil. Oxford Air Training School. CSE. TWR 118.875MHz, APP 130.3MHz

Kinloss (Grampian Reg) North side of B9089 just east of junction with B9011, off A96, 3 miles northeast of Forres. RAF Nos 120, 201, 206 Sqns Nimrods

Kirkwall (Orkney) Southeast of Kirkwall off A960. Civil. British Airways, Loganair schedules. Oil related charters. TWR 118.3MHz

Lakenheath (Suffolk) Five miles north of Barton Mills, west of A1065, east of B1112. USAF No 48TFW F-111Fs

Lasham (Hants) Five miles south of Basingstoke to east of A339, 4 miles northwest of Alton. Civil. Dan-Air maintenance base. Gliding centre

Leavesden (Herts) Two miles northwest of Watford at junction of A411, A41, A405 and M25. Civil. Light and executive aircraft. TWR 122.15MHz

Leeming (Yorks) East side of A1, south of A684 to Northallerton Nos 11 and 25 Sqn Tornados. Northumbrian UAS Bulldogs, No 11 AEF Chipmunks. TWR 122.1MHz, APP 127.75MHz

Lee-on-Solent (Hants) Four miles west of Gosport south of B3334, 3 miles south of Fareham. RN. HMS Daedalus. Helicopters, communications aircraft. Civil. Light aircraft. Gliders. Southampton UAS Bulldogs. TWR 135.7MHz

Leicester (Leics) Four miles east-southeast of city east of B667 connecting road between A47 and A6 near Stoughton. Civil. Light aircraft. A/G 122.25MHz

Leuchars (Fife Reg) Seven miles southeast of Dundee, east side of A919. RAF No 111 Sqn, No 228 OCU (No 64 Sqn) Phantoms, No 22 Sqn B Flt, SAR helicopters, Aberdeen, Dundee & St Andrews UAS Bulldogs

Lindholme (Yorks) Six miles northeast of Doncaster, east side of A614, 3 miles south of A18. RAF. RLG for Finningley. Gliders

Linton-on-Ouse (Yorks) West of A19 at Shipton, 10 miles northwest of York. Minor roads via Newton-on-Ouse to airfield. RAF. No 1 FTS. Jet Provosts. No 642 VGS Ventures. TWR 122.1MHz, App 129.15MHz

Little Snoring (Norfolk) Four miles northeast of Fakenham, 1 mile north of A148. Civil. Light aircraft

Little Staughton (Cambs) Four miles west of St Neots west of A45. Civil. Light aircraft

Llanbedr (Gwynedd) Three miles south of Harlech to west of A496. RAE. Sea Vixen, Meteor, Jindivik target drones. TWR 122.5MHz

Lossiemouth (Grampian Reg) West of B9135, west off A941, 5 miles north of Elgin. RAF No 8 Sqn Shackletons, Nos 12 and 208 Sqn, 237 OCU Buccaneers, Hunters, No 226 OCU Jaguars. No 202 Sqn D Flt SAR helicopters

Lyneham (Wilts) South of A420, 8 miles southwest from M4 Junction 16. RAF No 24, 30, 47 and 70 Sqns, 242 OCU Hercules. TWR 123.4MHz, APP 118.425MHz

Machrihanish/Campbeltown (Strathclyde Reg) Four miles west-northwest of Campbeltown, 2 miles west of A83. RAF. Used for exercises. Loganair services. APP 119.7MHz. TWR 122.1MHz

Marham (Norfolk) North of A1122 between Downham Market and Swaffham. RAF No 55 Sqn Victors, Nos 27 and 617 Sqn Tornados

Merryfield (Somerset) Between A358 and B3168 north of Ilminster. RN. Satellite for Yeovilton. Helicopters

Middle Wallop (Hants) Six miles southwest of Andover southeast of A343 at junction with B3084. AAC. Helicopters and light aircraft. Museum of Army Flying TWR 122.1MHz, APP 126.7MHz

Mildenhall (Suffolk) On south side of A1101 3 miles from A11 at Barton Mills. USAF transports and tankers,USN aircraft

Mona (Gwyedd) North side of A5, 9 miles west of Menai Bridge. RAF. Satellite for Valley. Light aircraft APP 134.35MHz

Netheravon (Wilts) Six miles north of Amesbury, 2 miles east of A345. AAC. Helicopters. Civil. Light aircraft

Netherthorpe (S. Yorks) Two miles southwest from A57, 3 miles northwest of Worksop. Civil. Light aircraft. A/G 123.5MHz

Newbury (Berks) One mile east of town off A34. Light aircraft, helicopters race days only

Newmarket Heath (Cambs) West of A1304 (old A11) south end of town. Light aircraft race days only

Newton (Notts) Eight miles east of Nottingham, north of A52, south of minor road, west of A46. RAF No 7 AEF Chipmunks, E Midlands UAS Bulldogs. TWR/APP 122.1MHz

Newtownards (N.Ireland) Off A20 southeast of town. Civil. Light aircraft. A/G 123.5MHz

Northholt (Greater London) North side of A40 west of junction with A4180, 2 miles east of Uxbridge. RAF. No 32 Sqn BAe 125, Andover, Gazelle. Civil executive visitors. TWR/APP 134.15MHz

North Ronaldsay (Orkney) Southwest side of island. Civil. Loganair services

North Weald (Essex) North side of B181,

south of A414, 2 miles northeast of Epping. Essex Gliding Club. Tugs. Aces High, The Squadron, Harvard Team, light aircraft A/G 123.525MHz

Nottingham/Tollerton (Notts) East of city to south of A52 and north of Tollerton village. Civil. Light aircraft. A/G 122.8MHz

Oban/Connel North (Strathclyde Reg) West of A828, 5 miles northeast of Oban. Civil. Air taxi and light aircraft

Odiham (Hants) Eight miles north of Alton to east of A32, 2 miles south of M3 Junction 5. RAF Nos 7 Sqn Chinooks, 33 Sqn Puma, 240 OCU

Old Sarum (Wilts) Two miles north of Salisbury to east of A345. AAC. Satellite for Middle Wallop. Civil. Light aircraft. Gliders. A/G 123.575MHz

Old Warden (Beds) Two miles west of Biggleswade signposted off A1 opposite junction with A6001 from east. Civil. Light aircraft. Shuttleworth Collection. A/G 123.05MHz

Oronsay (Strathclyde) South end of the island. Civil. Loganair flights

Panshanger (Herts) Four miles west of Hertford, south of B1000. West side of link road to A414 at Cole Green. Civil. Light aircraft. A/G 120.25MHz

Papa Stour (Shetland) On south side of island. Civil. Loganair flights

Papa Westray (Orkney) On west side of island. Civil. Loganair services

Perranporth (Cornwall) Ten miles northwest of Truro west of the B3285, southwest of village. Civil. Light aircraft, gliding centre

Perth/Scone (Tayside Reg) Four miles northeast of Perth west of A94. Civil. Air Service Training aircraft. TWR 119.8MHz, APP 122.3MHz

Peterborough/Conington (Cambs) Eight miles south of Peterborough, south of B660, east of A1. Civil. Light and company aircraft. A/G 129.725MHz

Peterhead (Grampian Reg) North of A950, 3 miles west of Peterhead. Civil. Light and company aircraft. Oil related charters. A/G 123.375MHz

Popham (Hants) North side of A30, 2 miles west of M3 Junction 8. Civil. Light aircraft. A/G 129.8MHz

Portland (Dorset) South of Weymouth to east of A354. RN. Helicopters. TWR 124.15MHz

Predannack (Cornwall) North of Lizard Point to west of A3083. RN. Satellite for Culdrose. Helicopters

Redhill (Surrey) Off minor road 2 miles south of A25, 1 mile east of town. Civil.

Light aircraft. Bristow Helicopters. A/G 123.225MHz

Rochester (Kent) Two miles south of town to west of A229 just north of M2 Junction 3. Civil. Light aircraft. A/G 122.25MHz

St Athan (S. Glam'n) Ten miles west of Barry to north of B4265. RAF MU. Wales UAS Bulldogs, No 634 VGS Vikings, museum aircraft

Samlesbury (Lancs) Six miles east of Preston between A59 and A677. British Aerospace. TWR 130.35MHz, APP 124.45MHz

Sanday (Orkney) Centre of island. Civil. Loganair services

Sandown (Isle of Wight) Two miles west of town, north of A3056. Civil. Light aircraft, ARV aircraft, microlights. A/G 123.5MHz

Scampton (Lincs) Six miles north of Lincoln, west of A15. RAF CFS Bulldogs, Gazelles, Hawks, Jet Provosts, Red Arrows Hawks, No 643 VGS Vikings

Sculthorpe (Norfolk) Four miles west of Fakenham, north of A148. USAF reserve base

Seething (Norfolk) Ten miles southeast of Norwich, south of village, east of minor road to B1135, 2 miles northwest of Bungay on A143. Civil. Light aircraft. A/G 122.6MHz

Shawbury (Salop) West side of B5063, north of A53, 9 miles northeast of Shrewsbury, RAF. Air Traffic School Jet Provosts, No 2 FTS Gazelles and Wessex, Bulldog MU. TWR/APP 122.1MHz

Sherburn (Yorks) Four miles east of A1, east of village south of B1222. Civil. Light aircraft. A/G 122.6MHz

Shipham (Norfolk) On north side of minor road southeast from A1075, 1 mile northeast of village and 4 miles south of East Dereham. Civil. Light aircraft. A/G 123.05MHz

Shobdon (Heref & Worc) Ten miles west of Leominster, south of village and B4362. Civil. Light aircraft. A/G 123.5MHz

Sibson (Cambs) Eight miles west of Peterborough, west of A1(T) east side of B671. Civil. Light aircraft. Parachute club. A/G 122.3MHz

Silverstone (N'hants) Seven miles northeast of Brackley to east of A43. Civil. Open on race days. Light aircraft, helicopters. A/G 121.075MHz

Skegness (Lincs) Two miles north of town, west side of A52. Civil. Light aircraft. A/G 130.45MHz

Sleap (Salop) Nine miles north of Shrewsbury, south of Wem west from B5476. Civil. Light aircraft. A/G 122.45MHz

South Marston (Wilts) Three miles northeast of Swindon, west side of minor road 1 mile north from A420, north of village. Civil. Light aircraft. A/G 129.9MHz

Stapleford (Essex) Five miles north of Romford, south of A113, west of junction with B175. Civil. Light and executive aircraft. A/G 122.8MHz

Stornoway (Hebrides) North of A866, 3 miles east of Stornoway. Civil. British Airways, Loganair services. Transit stop for aircraft on transatlantic delivery. TWR 123.5MHz

Strathallan (Tayside Reg) Three miles northwest of Auchterarder, to west of B8062. Civil. Light aircraft. Parachute Club. A/G 129.9MHz

Stronsay (Orkney) Northwest end of island north of B9062. Civil. Loganair services

Sturgate (Lincs) Five miles southeast of Gainsborough between A631 and B1241. Civil. Light aircraft. A/G 130.3MHz

Sumburgh (Shetland) Twenty miles from Lerwick at south of main island. Civil. British Airways, Loganair services. Bristow and British International Helicopters base. Oil industry charter traffic. TWR 118.25MHz, APP 123.15MHz

Swansea/Fairwood Common (W. Glamorgan) Six miles west of Swansea on A4118. Civil. Club, private and company operated aircraft. Helicopters. TWR/APP 119.7MHz

Swanton Morley (Norfolk) Four miles north-northeast of Dereham, 1 mile west of B1147 in Mill Street. RAF. Gliding centre, civil light aircraft. No 611 VGS Vikings. TWR 123.5MHz

Swinderby (Lincs) East side of A46, 7 miles northeast of Newark. RAF EFTS Chipmunks

Sywell (Northants) Five miles northeast of Northampton, east off A43 to north of village. Civil. Light aircraft. A/G 122.7MHz

Tatenhill (Staffs) Six miles west of Burton-on-Trent, 1 mile east of A515 south of B5234. Civil. Light and executive aircraft. Allied Breweries. A/G 122.2MHz

Ternhill (Salop) Southwest side of A41, southeast of junction with A53, 3 miles southwest of Market Drayton. RAF. RLG for Shawbury. TWR 124.15MHz

Thruxton (Hants) Six miles west of Andover, north of A303. Civil. Light aircraft, helicopters. A/G 130.45MHz

Thurleigh (Beds) Five miles north of Bedford, north of minor road towards B660, 2 miles east from A6 at Milton Ernest. RAE. Experimental and research aircraft. TWR 130.0MHz

Tingwall/Lerwick (Shetland) Five miles northwest of Lerwick, southwest of A971. Civil. Loganair services. A/G 122.6MHz

Tiree (Strathclyde) In centre of island north of B8065. Civil. Loganair services. TWR 122.7MHz

Tollerton (Notts) See Nottingham

Topcliffe (Yorks) East side of A167, 2 miles north of A168, 3 miles southwest of Thirsk. RAF. RLG for Linton-on-Ouse. AAC helicopters. No 1 FTS/RNEFTS Bulldogs. TWR 123.3MHz

Unst (Shetland) East of A968, 2 miles southeast of Baltasound. Civil. Loganair services. RAF communications aircraft. TWR/APP 130.35MHz

Upavon (Wilts) South side of A342, 2 miles east of junction with A345, 8 miles north of Amesbury. RAF. Gliders, helicopters, light aircraft. No 622 VGS Vikings

Upper Heyford (Oxon) Five miles west-northwest of Bicester, west of A43, north of B4030. USAF. 20 TFW F-111s, 66 ECW EF-111s

Valley (Gwynedd) Five miles southeast of Holyhead, 1 mile south of A5. RAF. No 4 FTS Hawks, No 22 Sqn C Flt, SAR helicopters APP 134.35MHz

Waddington (Lincs) Five miles south of Lincoln between A607 and A15. RAF No 8 Sqn Sentry

Warton (Lancs) On south side of A584, 4 miles east of Lytham. British Aerospace factory. Jaguars, Tornados. TWR 130.8MHz, APP 124.45MHz

Wattisham (Suffolk) Nine miles northwest of Ipswich, north side of B1078 from A45 at Needham Market. RAF. Nos 56 and 74 Sqn Phantoms. TWR 122.1MHz, APP 123.4MHz

Wellesbourne Mountford (Warwicks) South of B4086, 1 mile west of A429, 4 miles east of Stratford-upon-Avon. Civil. Light and company aircraft. A/G 130.45MHz

West Freugh (Dumfries) Five miles southeast of Stranraer, west side by junction of A715 and A757. RAE. Trials aircraft. Avionic systems testing. TWR 122.55MHz. APP 130.05MHz

West Malling (Kent) East of A228, 2 miles south of A20, 5 miles west of Maidstone. Civil. Light aircraft. No 618 VGS Vikings. Metair works. Saab SF340s. TWR 130.875MHz

Weston-super-Mare (Avon) Two miles southeast of town on west side of A371. No 621 VGS Vikings. Helicopter museum.

Westray (Orkney) North end of island. Civil. Loganair services

Wethersfield (Essex) East of B1053, 7 miles north-northwest of Braintree. No 614 VGS Vikings. USAF. Reserve base

Weybridge (Surrey) East of A318 south of Weybridge. Helicopters. A/G 122.35MHz

Whalsay (Shetland) Northeast end of island. Civil. Loganair services

White Waltham (Berks) Three miles southwest of Maidenhead, 1 mile south from A4 and A423(M) junction. Civil. Light aircraft. TWR 122.6MHz

Wickenby (Lincs) East of minor road 1 mile north of B1399, 1 mile east from A158, 10 miles northeast of Lincoln. Civil. Light aircraft. Crop sprayers. A/G 122.45MHz

Wittering (Northants) Three miles south of Stamford on west side of A1. RAF. No 1 Sqn and 233 OCU Harriers

Woodbridge (Suffolk) North side of minor road 2 miles east of B1083, 2 miles south of A1152. USAF 81TFW A-10A, 39 SOW C-130, MH-53

Woodford (Greater Manchester) Three miles east of Wilmslow south of A5102. British Aerospace. Nimrod, ATP and 146. TWR 126.925MHz, APP 130.05MHz

Woodvale (Merseyside) Five miles south-southwest of Southport west of A565. RAF. No 10 AEF Chipmunks. Liverpool UAS Bulldogs, Civil. Light aircraft. TWR 120.65MHz

Wroughton (Wilts) West side of minor road, south from B4005 1 mile east of A361, 3 miles south of Swindon. Science Museum Collection. RN. Helicopters

Wyburton (Lincs) Two miles west of Boston, north side of A1121 near junction with A52. Civil. Light aircraft. Crop sprayers

Wycombe Air Park See Booker

Wyton (Cambs) Three miles northeast of Huntingdon, east of Junction A141/B1090. RAF Nos 100, 360 Sqn, 231 OCU Canberras, 51 PRU Nimrods

Yeovil (Somerset) One mile southwest of town south of A3088. Westland factory. Helicopter production. TWR 125.4MHz, APP 130.8MHz

Yeovilton (Somerset) Two miles east of Ilchester south side of B3151 south of A303. RN. Hunters, Canberras, helicopters. Sea Harriers. FAA Museum, Concorde Hall

Sikorsky S-61N G-BCEB has been based at Penzance for many years. *AJW*

Top:
Prestwick has an excellent roof terrace but very few movements of note nowadays.
Worldways' DC-8 C-FCPQ is still a regular visitor, unlike the LOT IL-18 SP-LCK which
arrived with a special charter. *AJW*

Centre:
With the demolition of a hangar at Southampton, for the moment it is now easier to
photograph the daily Air France/Brit Air ATR-42 visitor, in this case F-GGLR. *AJW*

Above:
Stansted no longer has good vantage points for photography although it is possible to
acquire landing shots such as this of Conair's Airbus A300 OY-CNK. *AJW*